Leslie Linsley's
New Weekend Quilts

Leslie Linsley's
New Weekend Quilts

25 Quick and Easy Quilting Projects
You Can Complete in a Weekend

Leslie Linsley

HOME

A HOME BOOK
Published by the Penguin Group
Penguin Group (USA) Inc.
375 Hudson Street, New York, New York 10014, USA
Penguin Group (Canada), 90 Eglinton Avenue East, Suite 700, Toronto, Ontario M4P 2Y3, Canada
    (a division of Pearson Penguin Canada Inc.)
Penguin Books Ltd., 80 Strand, London WC2R 0RL, England
Penguin Group Ireland, 25 St. Stephen's Green, Dublin 2, Ireland (a division of Penguin Books Ltd.)
Penguin Group (Australia), 250 Camberwell Road, Camberwell, Victoria 3124, Australia
    (a division of Pearson Australia Group Pty. Ltd.)
Penguin Books India Pvt. Ltd., 11 Community Centre, Panchsheel Park, New Delhi—110 017, India
Penguin Group (NZ), Cnr. Airborne and Rosedale Roads, Albany, Auckland 1310, New Zealand
    (a division of Pearson New Zealand Ltd.)
Penguin Books (South Africa) (Pty.) Ltd., 24 Sturdee Avenue, Rosebank, Johannesburg 2196, South Africa

Penguin Books Ltd., Registered Offices: 80 Strand, London WC2R 0RL, England

While the author has made every effort to provide accurate telephone numbers and Internet addresses at the time of publication, neither the publisher nor the author assumes any responsiblity for errors, or for changes that occur after publication. Further, the publisher does not have any control over and does not assume any responsibility for author or third-party websites or their content.

First edition: November 2006

The Library of Congress Cataloging-in-Publication Data

Linsley, Leslie.
  Leslie Linsley's new weekend quilts : 25 quick and easy quilting projects you can complete in a weekend / Leslie Linsley.— 1st ed.
    p. cm
  ISBN 1-55788-495-1
1. Patchwork—Patterns. 2. Quilting—Patterns. I. Title II. Title: New weekend quilts.
TT835.L565153 2006
746.46'041—dc22

                                           2006023695

PRINTED IN THE UNITED STATES OF AMERICA

10 9 8 7 6 5 4 3 2 1

Most Home Books are available at special quantity discounts for bulk purchases for sales promotions, premiums, fund-raising, or educational use. Special books, or book excerpts, can also be created to fit specific needs. For details, write: Special Markets, The Berkley Publishing Group, 375 Hudson Street, New York, New York 10014.

Contents

Introduction

Gallery of Projects

Contents

Introduction

QUILTING: AN AMERICAN TRADITION

I have always been intrigued by the history of simple folk arts that evolved in response to specific needs. A good example is basketmaking, a craft developed for carrying and containing specific items. As the saying goes, "Necessity is the mother of invention," and quilt making was born out of necessity. Making bed covers was the most natural way for women to recycle worn clothing for keeping warm. Quilt making has been part of America's way of life since our country was first settled. Patchwork, the sewing together of fabric to fabric to create a pieced whole cloth, is the only needlework that is one of our earliest indigenous American crafts. And although quilting was done worldwide, nowhere else did it become the art form it is in this country. I don't think those early quilt makers ever thought of their needlework as an art, but simply as a means to an end.

Quilt making was tremendously popular in the latter half of the 1800s, so a great number of antique quilts stem from that period, many of which have survived in good condition. These quilts are among the most prized collectibles because of their wonderful designs and exquisite needlework.

While antique quilts are appreciated for their historic significance, artful design, and skillful craftsmanship, the increasing interest in these quilts comes from a desire to re-create the old patterns with new materials. Many people who can sew are intrigued by the idea of making their own quilts and quilted projects, and this interest has opened up a whole new realm of creativity for the home crafter. The projects are good-looking and useful, and with leisure time at a premium, making quilts provides a most satisfying creative outlet. The results are also significant in that they help to carry on an American tradition.

Today there is hardly anything that is handmade out of necessity. In fact not many things are handmade, especially for everyday use. Therefore, those early folk art items are so much more valuable and appreciated for their nostalgic qualities that represent a lifestyle quite removed from our own.

Over the past twenty years I've written several quilt books, but the very first one was the most popular. It was called *The Weekend Quilt*. The idea came to me while I was working for *Family Circle* magazine. Over the years my studio was responsible for designing craft projects for people who wanted to make something with their hands but had limited leisure time. Most of our projects, from faux finishing furniture to complete room makeovers, were designed for quick and easy crafting. Quilting was just becoming popular. I love fabric and the challenge of creating something useful and appealing by putting together different prints and shapes.

However, as a busy working mother, I knew how hard it was for people to finish such a project in a reasonable amount of time. The question I asked myself on behalf of my readers was, "Is it possible to create a design for making a quilt that can be pieced in a weekend?" I remember designing and making that quilt in our studio and the feeling that I was on to something that would become a unique concept. At the time, country style was at its peak and a quilt was the perfect accessory for creating country warmth in any room. If you wanted to give an expression of love to new parents or newlyweds, nothing could be more perfect than a quilt. Further, antique quilts were out of the closet, so to speak, as valuable American folk art for collectors. Suddenly names like Bear Claw, Log Cabin, and Ohio Star were familiar to anyone who knew anything about quilts. Quilting classes were springing up in towns across America, and people flocked to learn how to reproduce and thus keep alive the patterns originally created by our earliest settlers.

Still, the biggest problem was committing to the time needed to make a quilt. Many women who wanted to quilt were simply too busy for this craft. They were dealing with commitments to work and running a household, and while many expressed a desire to quilt, there just wasn't enough time left over in the week.

It was Labor Day Weekend when we hit on the idea. My husband and partner, Jon Aron, and I were in the studio designing a quilt pattern that could be made with iron-on seam binding. The magazine often asked us to come up with innovative ideas for creating craft projects with a twist. We decided to create a patchwork quilt that could be pieced in a weekend. The quilt that we designed ended up on the cover of the magazine and the response to the article was so overwhelming that it led to my first quilt book, *The Weekend Quilt*. That book was the beginning of the craze for all sorts of craft books and articles that followed, with the main idea being to save time and create a project from start to finish in a weekend.

We decided to use novices, people who had never before made a quilt but felt comfortable sewing a straight line on a sewing machine. Early American patchwork quilt patterns are based on geometric shapes such as squares, rectangles, and triangles, so most patchwork designs require little more knowledge than that. We then designed nineteen quilts, devising shortcuts and quick and easy techniques for ensuring that each quilt could be successfully pieced in a weekend. After that we reworked the designs, redesigning many of them to work within the premise. We also visited fabric showrooms to become familiar with the most up-to-date materials best suited for quilts. We arranged and rearranged colors and adjusted sizes so that the same patterns could be adapted to different bed sizes. Finally, we received much help in the form of information about products carried by various manufacturers to ease the quilt-making process. The results were then combined into the completion of nineteen quilts.

The novice quilters who made the quilts used our shortcuts and machine-stitched all the patchwork pieces for the quilt tops. We asked them to keep notes about the patterns and directions so that we could revise and perfect them. The quilters had six months to complete their quilts, but the overall time spent on crafting could not exceed sixteen hours. When the tops were completed, they could then add the batting and backing and use the quilt as is or take their time hand-quilting at their leisure. When they had completed their quilts, many of them wanted to make another using one of the other patterns, and ultimately formed a quilting bee to meet on a regular basis. Three went on a vacation together and used the time to quilt. And so our original weekend quilters quickly became hooked for longer periods.

This got me thinking about offering suggestions in my future books for forming a quilting club. Just as those early American women got together to quilt, it could be fun and quite satisfying for a group of contemporary women to get together to socialize while creating something with their hands. They might work on individual quilts or a quilt to be donated to a worthy cause. Another reason to make a quilt together might be to jointly create a special gift when someone's daughter or son was about to be married. While researching ideas for a quilting bee, I discovered that a trend among new mothers is to enjoy a night out with other women in their situation, while working on quilt projects. Getting together to talk about baby problems while working on baby quilts can be a lot of fun. Other groups of young college women are getting together in sorority houses to make quilts for fund-raising and to make small gifts. "As long as the projects are simple, inexpensive, and don't take much time," a University of South Carolina student told me, "we love to craft."

Over the years I've learned about other groups of quilters who get together to do good works. They make quilts to donate for church and school and other fund-raising events. They make quilts to give to hospitals. There are groups of quilters all over the country making quilts to raise money for cancer and AIDS research, and there are quilt makers sending quilts overseas so that our servicemen and women can wrap themselves in the warmth of a handmade gift.

It's been many years since *The Weekend Quilt* was first published, and it seems clear that there's a new generation of potential quilters with the same aim—to make a quilt without committing an endless amount of time to complete it. Women today have even less time than they did ten or fifteen years ago, and materials, designs, and products have improved. So, when I was asked to produce a new and improved version of the original book using the weekend concept, it presented me with an interesting challenge. The quilting projects in this book were designed for beginners; however, we think they will interest the busy experienced crafter as well. While the projects here might be easy to do, I think you'll find a variety of good-looking items to choose from and the end results will be worthy of your time.

Since the same patterns have been passed down through the generations, variations on each have evolved. Along the way, many quilters have solved basic problems by devising easier methods that benefit those who follow them. The choices of fabric colors are yours, so you can feel free to be creative with the patterns shown here by matching colors to your decorating scheme. Use the outlines of the patterns and a variety of colored pencils to try different color schemes before buying your material. In this way you can see how different colors work together in the pattern to form the completed design. Or buy small amounts of fabric and cut tiny pattern pieces to glue to paper to see how these fabrics look together in the quilt pattern.

Basically we started with original early American patterns and devised even more innovative shortcuts and fabric with up-to-date colors and prints to re-create the most popular quilts. Add to this many suggestions for how to form a quilting club and we think you'll be on your way to your first quilting project or, if you are a seasoned quilter, to a variety of design ideas for your next project. Who knows? You might even learn a new trick or two. And if you discover any shortcuts in the course of your quilting experience, please send them along to me so that I can, in turn, pass them along in subsequent books. Such is the nature of quilt making. It is a forever craft for creating future family treasures.

Leslie Linsley
Nantucket, MA
leslie@leslielinsley.com

FORMING A QUILTING CLUB

Quilting has once again become a full-blown American craft. I say "once again" because quilting has always been an American tradition, but every few years it becomes a craze, a trend, a way of life. Craft shops, once devoted to other crafts, are suddenly "quilt shops" exclusively.

Today's quilting clubs all over the country are much the same as they were back in colonial days. Church members have always formed groups in order to make a fund-raising quilt to raffle off. We have 4H clubs and Homemaker's Extension groups that include quilting as one of their main activities. There are quilting bees with as few as six members and national organizations with hundreds of members. Quilting is being taught in elementary schools as well as high school home economics classes. There are books and home learning tapes on how to do patchwork and appliqué and how to master various quilting techniques. Quilters' newsletters abound. There are mail-order sources for everything needed to make a quilt, and whether you live in a rural area or a big city, there's a good chance that you'll find a group of avid quilters eager to form a regular quilting get-together.

Approaching two or three friends who want to devote an hour or two each week for socializing and sewing is probably the easiest way to get started. The first, or introductory, meeting will be for the purpose of planning your individual quilt projects or one project that everyone will work on together. Once the project or projects are determined, you will make a date for the next meeting. By the second meeting everyone should have purchased their fabrics and the necessary materials, such as pins, ruler, scissors, and so on. Wherever the gathering is held, there should be a table large enough to measure and cut the fabric for each quilt. The next meeting would involve pinning pieces together to prepare for piecing, which each person will do on her own using her sewing machine. If there is only one sewing machine in the group, each person can take a turn using it while the others are working on another step of the process.

Another way to join a quilting club is through a local fabric shop. Many fabric shops have regular get-togethers for quilting, and if they don't, they would probably like to put something together with your help. If it's more desirable to get together in your own home, the fabric shop might let you put up a notice to solicit a small group of interested people.

When I started this book, I interviewed several quilters who belong to a group. One of the women is a member of an Indiana homemakers' group. As a proud American, she voiced heartfelt sentiments I heard again and again. She said, "I remember as a young girl sitting under the dining room table and listening to my mother and her sisters (my aunts) talking. It was my 'private' house because they were working on a quilt and the fabric was spread over the table and spilled down onto the floor. They never knew I was there, but later when

I was old enough, they let me thread the needles for them so they wouldn't have to stop what they were doing. I remember how proud I was when I was able to join that group of women to make a quilt for the church raffle. Today, as a fourth-generation quilter, I feel so proud and lucky to have such a fine heritage. It is one that I am now passing on to my daughters, and even my son has begun to get interested. I dream of quilt patterns and know that I will never live long enough to complete every project I've dreamed up."

And from another quilter in Kentucky, "I love the words to our national anthem and found a group of women with sons and daughters in the service. We decided to get together to make patriotic quilts to send overseas. It is such a wonderful thing to be able to honor our country in such a personal way." One of the quilters I met was a Native American, who said, "I always have a quilting square in my lap. Quilting is part of my life. Everything I do, every major event, is commemorated in my quilts. When my children leave home to begin their new lives without me, I want them to take a piece of their past with them and this will be in the form of a quilt." A new mother had this to say, "I love knowing that once a week I have this special time with my friends where we're all making crib quilts for our babies. When one of our friends or family is pregnant, we all work on one quilt to give as a joint gift. This time has become so special to me and we have all grown closer through this experience."

My assistant, Lauren, just graduated from college. She and her friends get together to make shower gifts and quilted pillows for their new homes. "It's great to be able to make a quilt or pillow from scraps of fabric that don't cost anything," she says. "I just finished a quilted pillow using the colors of my sorority house. Now all my friends want to make one as well."

I interviewed two quilters living in my hometown. They are typical of today's young women, juggling home, career, marriage, and parenting. They also find time for quilt making together because it relieves the stress that often comes from a hectic schedule. One of the women is a teacher and has taught her two young sons to quilt. "They absolutely loved it," she told me. "I taught them all about the quilting steps and the background of quilting and they were fascinated. They couldn't wait to get at the sewing machine," she added.

Throughout the book you will find tips for breaking down the quilting steps for each project, making it simple and convenient to quilt with others. There are also tips for shortcuts to various steps. Whether you quilt with one friend or many, you'll be able to work on one quilt for the common cause that you've agreed upon, or you can use the same pattern to make your own individual projects. You'll be able to have fun choosing your own colors and prints to go with your décor and see how the same pattern can look completely different with these color and fabric variations. Quilt making is fun. Quilt making is infectious. Quilt making relieves stress. Quilt making is useful. And best of all, you will be creating tomorrow's heirlooms for future generations.

QUILTING TERMS

The "language" of quilting is employed throughout this book to describe the various steps used to make the projects. It is easily learned and will help you to understand the different processes involved in making any quilt project. This information will also help you to understand the projects' directions. They are basic and logical, and if you are new to the craft, they will enable you to see how easy it is. Take the time to read this information before starting a project. It will give you an overview of what's to come, and will probably save you time and errors as you proceed. Then, from time to time, you can refer back to specific information when a particular direction suggests doing so. This will make each set of project directions easier to understand.

Backing

The piece of fabric used on the underside of the pieced top of a project. Usually of the same-weight fabric, this piece can be made from solid or printed fabric to match the top design. Sometimes the backing is made from the same fabric as that used to create borders on a quilt or wall hanging. I especially like to use a sheet for the backing on a quilt. The sizes are large enough without adding seams for piecing. When making small projects, one of the fabric pieces from the top can be used for the backing. In this way the project is completely coordinated.

Basting

Securing the top, batting, and backing together with long loose stitches before quilting. These stitches are removed after each section is quilted.

Batting

The soft lining that makes a quilt puffy and gives it warmth. Most quilts are made with a thin layer of Poly-Fil. This thin layer of batting is also used between the top and backing of a pillow that is being quilted. Batting comes in various thicknesses, each appropriate for different kinds of projects. It also comes in small, fluffy pieces that are used for stuffing smaller projects such as sachets, pincushions, pillows, and so on.

Binding

The way the raw edges of fabric are finished. Many quilt makers cut the backing slightly larger than the top piece so they can bring the extra fabric forward to finish the edges. Contrasting fabric or bias binding is also used.

Block

This is often referred to as a square. Geometric or symmetrical pieces of fabric are sewn together to create a design. The finished blocks are then joined to create the finished quilt top. Individual blocks are often large enough to use for a matching pillow. A series of small blocks can be joined to create an interesting pattern for a wall hanging.

Borders

Fabric strips that frame the pieced design. A border can be narrow or wide, and sometimes there is more than one border around a quilt, pillow, or wall hanging. Borders often frame quilt blocks and are sometimes made from one of the fabrics or from a contrasting fabric. Borders are often used to extend the size of a quilt top so that it drops down over the sides of the mattress.

Traditionally, quilting patterns are stitched in the borders of a quilt for interest. However, many quilters leave this area free of stitches in order to complete the project in a shorter period of time. When making small projects, a quilting pattern often adds interest to the patchwork top.

Patchwork

Sewing together of fabric pieces to create an entire design. Sometimes the shapes form a geometric block. The blocks are then sewn together to create the completed project.

Piecing

Joining patchwork pieces together to form a design on the block.

Quilting

Stitching together two layers of fabric with a layer of batting between.

Quilting Patterns

The lines or markings on the fabric that make up the design. Small hand or machine stitches follow along these lines, which might be straight or curved or made up of elaborate curlicue patterns. Small quilting stitches can follow the seam lines where pieces of fabric are joined. A quilting pattern can also be created by stitching a grid or pattern of diamonds over the entire fabric.

Sashes or Strips

The narrow pieces of fabric used to frame the individual blocks and join them together. They are often created in a contrasting color.

Setting

Joining the quilt blocks to form the finished top piece of a quilt.

Template

A pattern that is rigid and full size. It can be cut from cardboard or plastic and is used to trace the design elements. Some quilters use sandpaper for their templates because they are of the acceptable weight and won't slide on the fabric. When cutting the fabric, you will usually add ¼ inch for seam allowance. All patterns used to make templates in this book include a seam allowance.

Top

A quilt's front layer of fabric with the right side showing. Patchwork pieces create the top fabric.

MATERIALS YOU'LL NEED

Fabric

You can never have too many different fabric patterns when designing a quilting project. Fabric is the main concern: what kind, how much to buy, and what colors or prints will work together.

Almost every type of fabric can be used for making quilts and quilting projects. However, most quilters prefer cotton and, if necessary, will settle for a cotton-polyester blend in order to find the right color or pattern for the project. All fabric should be washed before it is used. This removes any sizing in the fabric and allows for shrinkage.

When collecting a variety of fabric prints for your quilting projects, it's a good idea to have a selection of lights and darks. The colors and patterns of the fabric will greatly affect the design. Calico is traditionally a favorite for quilting projects. The small, overall prints can be used effectively together and there is a wide variety of colors to choose from. If you are making a quilt for a specific room, you might have leftover fabric from upholstery or drapes and curtains to use for a coordinated project. Choose colors to go with your room décor.

Needles

The patchwork pieces used for the projects in this book are stitched together on a sewing machine. The quilting can be done by hand or on the machine. If stitching by hand, you will need #7 and #8 sharps, which are the most common sizes used for hand quilting. They are often called "betweens."

Thread

Match the thread to the color of the fabric for piecing on the machine. Cotton or cotton-blend threads are preferred by most quilters. The hand stitching is almost always done with white threads.

Scissors

Good-quality scissors are essential for accurately cutting your fabric. Do not use your fabric scissors for cutting paper. This will ruin your scissors.

Thimble

When hand quilting, you will be taking 3 to 6 stitches at a time through 3 layers of fabric. It takes a while to get used to using a thimble, but most quilters find it makes the process more fun—and less painful.

Iron

Have you ever known anyone to sew without an iron next to the sewing machine? It's impossible to do without it. It's handy to pad a stool or chair with a piece of batting and place it next to you by the sewing machine. As you piece the fabric, you can iron the seams without getting up. Use a steam setting.

Cutting Board

This is a handy item for the quick measuring and cutting methods you'll use for making the quilting projects in this book. It is available in fabric stores or from mail order sources. Some cutting boards are divided into a grid for easy measuring. Some have a ruler attached, others are plain.

Cutting Wheel

A cutting wheel is a useful and inexpensive tool for cutting strips of fabric for strip piecing. It is used by placing a metal straight edge on the fabric and running the circular blade of the cutting wheel along the side of the straight edge.

Ruler and Yardstick

These are a must. A metal ruler can be used as a straight edge for your most accurate cutting. Use the yardstick for cutting lengths of fabric where you must mark and cut at least 36 inches at one time.

The width of the yardstick is often used to mark a grid pattern for quilting. You simply draw the first line, then flip the yardstick over and continue to mark lines without ever removing the yardstick from the fabric. You will have a perfect 1-inch grid.

Ripper

This isn't something we like to anticipate using, but it is inevitable that even the best stitcher will make an error. Some people find this a handy tool. I prefer sharp snipping scissors, which are also used to trim loose threads at the beginning and end of piecing.

QUILTING TECHNIQUES

Estimating Amount of Fabric

The fabric used for all the projects is 45-inches wide. All measurements are figured with a ¼-inch seam allowance.

If a quilt size for any project shown here isn't the right size for your bed, it can be changed by adding to, or subtracting from, the border measurements. This shouldn't change the basic design.

The amounts of material needed for all projects in the book have been figured out and listed at the beginning of each project. It's always a good idea to buy a little extra to allow for any cutting or stitching errors.

Piecing the Backing

You may have to piece panels together for the back of a quilt or wall hanging in order to get the correct size. Use the full width of fabric, usually 45 inches, cut to the appropriate length. Cut another piece the same size. Then cut the second strip of fabric in half lengthwise so that you have two narrow strips the same size. Join these two matching panels to each long-sided edge of the large, center panel to avoid a seam down the middle of the quilt backing. Press seams open.

Enlarging a Design

If you'd like to enlarge the size of a quilt or wall hanging, there are several approaches, but the most important thing to remember is to buy enough extra material to accommodate the increased size. If the project is made up of a series of connecting blocks, simply add more quilt blocks to each row in either direction. Or you can add a border around the outside. If a border is part of the original design, make it wider or add another border in another coordinated fabric.

Cutting

Before cutting out each pattern piece, especially where long strips and borders are called for, carefully plan the layout of the pieces on the fabric. You do not want to begin by cutting the smallest pieces and end up without enough fabric for the larger pieces.

Making a Template

You can use oak tag, cardboard, or acetate to make a template.

If you use oak tag or cardboard, you'll have to transfer the pattern to the template material by first tracing the design with a soft pencil. Place the tracing facedown on the cardboard and rub over each traced line with a pen or a pencil. The outline will be transferred to the cardboard. Remove the tracing and go over the lines with a ballpoint pen to make them clearer. Cut out the design outline from the cardboard. If you use acetate, simply place it over the tracing and cut out the exact shape.

There are several advantages to using acetate for your template material. It can be used many times without losing its sharp edges, and since it's clear, you can trace a pattern piece directly onto it. Further, you can see through it when placing it on your fabric in order to position it where you want it. In this way, if you are using a floral print, for example, you might want to center a flower in the middle of the template piece. Draw a line from point to point on your template to make positioning more accurate.

Cutting Squares, Rectangles, and Triangles

To determine the cut size for simple shapes, use the following quide:

> *Squares:* Add ½ inch to the finished size.
> *Rectangles:* Add ½ inch to the finished length and width.
> *Half-square triangles:* Add ⅞ inch to the finished short side of the triangle. Cut a square that size and cut it on the diagonal to make 2 half-square triangles.
> *Quarter-square triangles:* Add 1¼ inches to the finished long side of the triangle. Cut a square that size and cut it twice diagonally to make 4 quarter-square triangles.

Quilting Techniques

HOW TO QUILT

Quilting is the means by which you sew layers of fabric and batting together to produce a padded fabric held together by stitching. The quilting process, generally the finishing step in patchwork projects, is what makes a project interesting and gives it a textured look.

Basting

Before quilting, you will baste the quilt top, batting, and backing together. To avoid a lump of filler at any point, begin at the center of the top and baste outward with long, loose stitches, thus creating a sunburst pattern. There should be about 6 inches between the basted lines at the edges of the quilt. Baste from the top only. These stitches will be cut away as you do your quilting.

Hand Quilting

Thread your needle and knot one end as for regular hand sewing. Bring the needle up through the back to the front and give the knotted end a good tug to pull it through the backing fabric into the batting. Keep your thread fairly short (about 18 inches) and take small running stitches. Follow your premarked quilting pattern.

Machine Quilting

This quicker way to create a quilted look does not have the same rich look of authentic, early quilting, which is hand-stiched. It is best to machine-quilt when the batting isn't too thick. Although the piecing of these quilts can be finished in a weekend, I still recommend hand quilting in a leisurely fashion unless it's more important that the project be completed quickly.

When machine quilting, set the thread tension at approximately 6 stitches to the inch so that the stitching looks like hand stitching. Taking this precaution will ensure that the absence of hand stitching does not detract from the design.

Outline Quilting

This is the method of quilting along the patchwork seams. In this way, each design element is pronounced and the layers of fabric are secure.

Overall Quilting

When you want to fill large areas of the background with quilting, choose a simple design. The background quilting should not interfere with the patchwork elements.

To ensure accurate spacing, make grid patterns of squares or diamond shapes with a yardstick or masking tape. For a quick and easy method, lay a yardstick diagonally across the fabric and mark the material with a light pencil. Without removing the yardstick, turn it over and mark along the edge once again. Continue across the fabric to the opposite edge. You will have perfect 1-inch spaces between each line. Lay the yardstick across the fabric at the corner, opposite where you began, and repeat the process to create a 1-inch grid across the top of the fabric. Stitch along these lines. The stitching will hide the pencil lines.

QUICK AND EASY METHODS

Strip Piecing

This is the method by which you sew strips of different fabrics together and then cut them into units that are arranged to make up the entire quilt top. (See Figure A.) Rather than cutting and sewing individual squares together over and over again, two or more strips of fabric are sewn together and then cut into segments that are of the exact same dimensions. These units are then arranged and stitched together in different positions to form the quilt pattern.

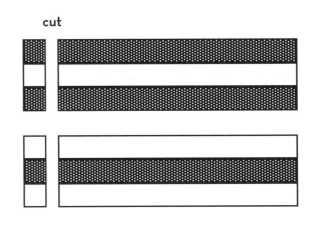

Figure A. Strip piecing.

Quick and Easy Triangle Method

This is a quick and easy way to join light and dark triangles to create two-color squares of any size. (See Figure B.) Once you've determined the size of your finished unit, add 1 inch to it. For example, if you want to create 2-inch squares, mark off 3-inch squares on the wrong side of the light fabric. Next, draw diagonal lines through each square as shown in Figure B. With right sides facing and raw edges aligned, pin the marked light fabric to the same-size dark fabric. Stitch a ¼-inch seam on each side of the drawn diagonal lines as shown in Figure B.

Cut on all solid lines to get the individual squares of light and dark, or contrasting fabric triangles. Press seams to the dark side.

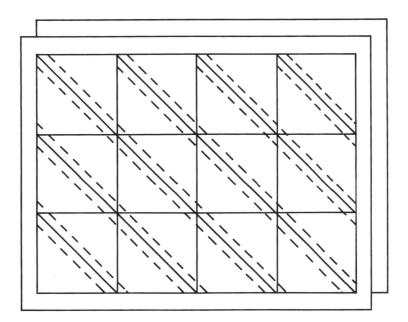

Figure B. Quick and easy triangle method.

Assembly Line Piecing

When a project calls for a series of the same types of pieces, especially small squares approximately 1 to 1½ inches, there's an easy method for stitching them together. With right side facing, pin individual sets of two squares each together. Stitch along one side edge but do not cut the thread when you reach the end. Leave the pressure foot down and run the machine for two or three more stitches and then feed the next set of squares through. Continue to stitch all the sets of squares in this way so you have a string of patches connected by threads between. When you have enough for the project, cut the strings between the squares to separate them. Open each set of squares and press. It's easy to sew them through the machine one right after the other rather than one at a time.

Pressing

Quilters are divided on the issue of whether to press seams open or to one side. Many believe that a quilt is stronger if seams are pressed to one side. However, if you are making a wall hanging or a quilt that will not get much wear and tear, the pieced top will look neater if the seams are pressed open. If the piecing has been done on the machine, it will have enough strength to withstand repeated washings no matter how the seams are pressed. If you are using light and dark fabrics stitched together, it is always best to press the seams to the dark side so the fabric doesn't show through. The important thing is to press seams each time you stitch fabric pieces together.

FINISHING TOUCHES

Adding Pillow Piping

Contrasting or matching piping is a nice way to finish the edges of a pillow. It gives the project a crisp and professional look when trimmed with matching fabric-covered piping. The piping can be very narrow, as for a small sachet, or quite fat, if used on an oversized throw pillow. The cording for piping is sold by the yard in most fabric shops and is quite inexpensive. It looks like soft rope.

Measure around the pillow edge and add an extra inch. Cut lengths of bias fabric 1½ inches wide and stitch together to create a strip long enough to go around the pillow, plus an extra inch.

Turn the short, raw edges of the fabric strip under ¼ inch and press. Cut the cording strip 1 inch shorter than the strip of fabric and place it in the center of the strip. Fold the fabric over the cording so the long, raw edges are aligned with the cord encased inside.

Using a zipper foot on your sewing machine, stitch along the fabric as close to the cording as possible. Do not stitch the last ½ inch of the fabric together. The cording will not reach the end of the fabric.

Begin at the center of one edge of the pillow top and pin piping all around with raw edges aligned. Where the two ends meet, overlap the extra fabric so that the cording comes together inside the fabric channel. Stitch around.

With right sides facing and raw edges aligned, pin the backing fabric piece to the top with the piping between. Stitch around 3 sides and 4 corners, leaving a few inches open on one side for turning. Trim the seam allowance and clip off the corners. Turn right side out and finish the pillow as directed in the project.

Slip Stitch

Once the pillow is stuffed with Poly-Fil or a pillow form, the easiest way to close the open side is with the slip stitch. Fold under the seam allowance on one side of the opening and pin it over the raw edges of the opposite side of the fabric.

Insert the needle through the bottom layer of the fabric right at the seam line at one end of the opening. Take a small stitch through the fold on the top layer, then through the seam line on the bottom layer. Continue in this way so that the seam line matches the area that has been machine-stitched from the wrong side.

Zipper

For easy removal of the pillow cover, a zipper can be stitched to the open side, rather than closing with a slip stitch. The directions for inserting a zipper are on the package. Buy a zipper in a color to match your fabric, and make sure it is 2 inches shorter than the length of the finished pillow.

Gallery of Projects

1: SHOO-FLY QUILT

It's interesting to think that a simple phrase like "Shoo fly!" would become the name for a classic early American quilt pattern. Perhaps the first one was so named because one of the pattern pieces looked like a fly swatter. Or perhaps more plausibly, the name evolved because the quilter was bothered by a fly while piecing together her quilt. This was often how early quilters named their patterns. This traditional 9-patch block quilt pattern has been repeated in many different colors by many generations of quilters, and it can look completely different depending on the colors and print combinations used.

To give this quilt a patriotic feeling, we made it in red, white, and blue in a square for hanging on a wall. The finished project is 61 × 61 inches. If you want to adjust the size to fit a bed, add more squares to one end and adjust the width of the border strips.

MATERIALS

All fabric is 45 inches wide.
1 yard solid blue fabric
1 yard white fabric
2 yards blue and white print fabric
4 yards red printed fabric
quilt batting cut 61 × 61 inches
tracing paper
cardboard or acetate

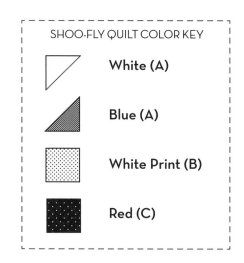

SHOO-FLY QUILT COLOR KEY

White (A)

Blue (A)

White Print (B)

Red (C)

DIRECTIONS

All measurements include a ¼-inch seam allowance.

1. Trace Patterns A and B (Figures 1 and 2), and transfer to cardboard to make templates. Seam allowance is included.
2. Using Pattern A, cut out 64 pieces from the solid blue fabric and 64 pieces from the white fabric.

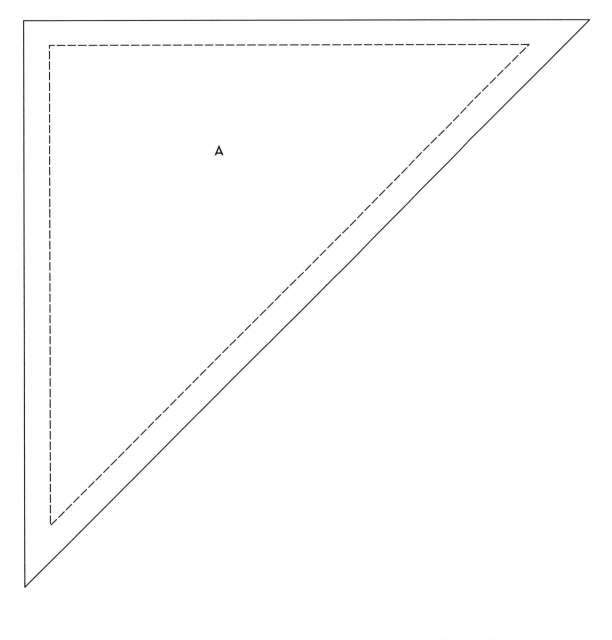

A

Figure 1. Pattern A.

Figure 2. Pattern B.

3. Using Pattern B, cut 64 blue and white print squares, each 5½ × 5½ inches.
4. Using Pattern B, cut 16 red squares, each 5½ × 5½ inches.
5. Cut red print for backing piece, 64 × 64 inches.
6. With right sides facing and raw edges aligned, join all blue and white triangle pieces along the long edge to create 64 squares. Press seams to dark side.

TO MAKE A BLOCK

Each block is made up of 9 squares joined together as shown in Figures 3 and 4.

1. Refer to Figure 3. With right sides facing and raw edges aligned, join an A square to a B square, followed by another A square. The A squares are all placed so that the white half of the fabric is in the outer corner. Open seams and press.
2. Next, join a B piece with a C piece, followed by another B piece. Press seams to one side.
3. Make a third row of 3 patches by joining an A piece with a B piece, followed by another A piece. Remember to place the A squares with the white half of the fabric in the outer corners. Open seams and press.
4. Refer to Figure 4. With right sides facing and raw edges aligned, join all 3 rows to make the 9-patch square.

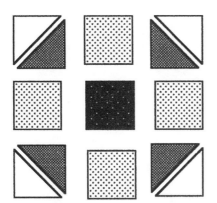

Figure 3. Make squares and
lay out pieces.

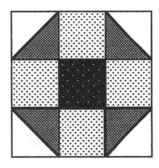

Figure 4. Assemble block.

Figures 3 and 4. Make a block.

TO MAKE ROWS

1. Refer to Figure 5. With right sides facing and raw edges aligned, join 2 blocks at one side edge. Open seams and press.
2. Add 2 more blocks in this way to create Row 1.
3. Continue to make 4 rows of 4 blocks each in this way as shown.

Figure 5. Join rows.

TO ASSEMBLE

1. Refer to Figure 6. With right sides facing and raw edges aligned, pin Row 1 to Row 2 along the bottom edge. Stitch across. Open seams and press.
2. Continue until you have stitched together 4 rows of 4 blocks each. Open seams and press.

Figure 6. Assembled rows.

TO QUILT

1. Pin the batting to the back of the patchwork top so there is 1-inch extra batting all around. This extra batting extends beyond the fabric to account for the border that will be added later. Baste the fabric and batting loosely together.
2. Using small running stitches, quilt ¼ inch from each side of each seam line. Remove basting stitches when quilting is complete.

TO FINISH

1. Place the quilted top over the wrong side of the backing fabric so that the backing extends 1½ inches beyond the top.
2. Turn backing edges forward ¼ inch and press all around.
3. Fold turned edges forward to cover the raw edges of the quilt top. Press and pin all around.
4. Stitch backing, which is now a 1-inch border, around the quilt top. You can hand-stitch with a slip stitch or machine-stitch to finish. See Figure 7 for the finished Shoo-Fly Quilt.

Figure 7. Finished Shoo-Fly Quilt with borders attached.

2: BABY'S FIRST QUILT

The announcement that a new baby is due is cause for celebration—and a wonderful excuse to make a baby quilt. My daughter Robby made this quilt. She lives on Cape Cod and is in the boating business, so a nautical color theme seemed appropriate.

This is an easy pattern to make as a first project if you are a beginning quilter. The squares are tied rather than quilted, but you can add hand quilting if you're not in a rush to finish the project. If you are making the quilt with a partner, you can divide up the squares (there are two different patchwork square patterns) so you will each have 15, rather than 30, blocks to put together. The finished size is 34 × 42 inches, making it ample for a carriage and a nice size for the crib.

MATERIALS

All fabric is 45 inches wide.
1¼ yards blue calico
1¾ yards bleached muslin
quilt batting, 34 × 42 inches
1 skein blue embroidery floss
tracing paper
cardboard or acetate

DIRECTIONS

All measurements and patterns include a ¼-inch seam allowance.

1. Trace Patterns A and B (Figure 1) and transfer them to cardboard to make templates. Seam allowance is included.
2. Cut the following:

    From blue:
        2 strips, each 3 × 35 inches (for top and bottom borders)
        2 strips, each 4½ × 34½ inches (side borders)

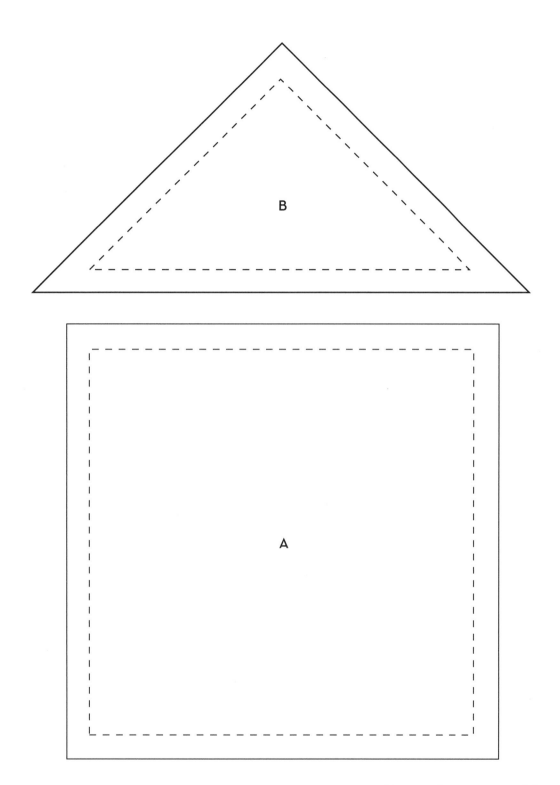

Figure 1. Patterns A and B.

15 squares using Pattern A
60 triangles using Pattern B

From muslin:
1 piece, 34¼ × 43 inches (backing)
15 squares using Pattern A
60 triangles using Pattern B

TO MAKE BLOCKS

Block 1
1. Refer to Figure 2. Join the diagonal edge of a muslin B piece to each edge of a blue A piece to make a Block 1.
2. Make 15 blocks in this way.

Block 2
1. Refer to Figure 2. Join the diagonal edge of a blue B piece to each edge of a muslin A piece to make a Block 2.
2. Make 15 blocks in this way.

Block 1   Block 2

Figure 2. Blocks 1 and 2.

TO MAKE ROWS

1. Refer to Figure 3. With right sides facing together, join a Block 1 to a Block 2 along one side edge.
2. Continue with another Block 1, then a Block 2, and end with another Block 1. Make 3 rows in this way for Rows 1, 3, and 5.
3. Refer to Figure 4. To make Rows 2, 4, and 6, join a Block 2 to a Block 1.
4. Continue with a Block 2, then another Block 1, and end with a Block 2.
5. Make 3 rows in this way.

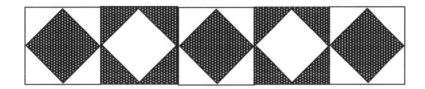

Figure 3. Make Rows 1, 3, and 5.

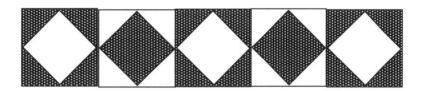

Figure 4. Make Rows 2, 4, and 6.

TO JOIN ROWS

1. With right sides facing and raw edges aligned, pin and stitch the bottom edge of Row 1 to the top edge of Row 2.
2. Continue to join all 6 rows in this way.

TO JOIN BORDERS

1. With right sides facing and raw edges aligned, pin a 3 × 34½-inch strip to the top edge of the quilt and stitch across. Open seams and press.
2. Repeat on the bottom edge.
3. Join a 4½ × 35-inch border strip to each side edge of the quilt in the same way to complete the quilt top.

TO TIE QUILT

1. With wrong sides together and batting between, pin top, batting, and backing fabric together.
2. Using 3 strands of embroidery floss approximately 12 inches long, tie the quilt through all layers at the center of each block and at each corner of each block in the following way: Bring needle down through layers to back and up again in the same place. Tie in a knot and cut ends of floss to within an inch of the knot.

TO FINISH

1. Trim batting to ¼ inch smaller than the quilt top all around.
2. Trim backing to the same size as the quilt top.
3. Turn the raw edges of the backing and quilt top to the wrong side ¼ inch and press. Pin in place.
4. Machine-stitch the pressed edges all around to close. See Figure 5 for the finished Baby's First Quilt.

Figure 5. Finished Baby's First Quilt.

3: IRISH CHAIN QUILT

This is a popular early quilt pattern created solely with square pieces of fabric. The two different fabric squares make up a 9-patch block. The Irish Chain is the perfect quilt pattern for strip piecing and is one of the easiest projects to make. The finished size is 63 × 81 inches. Since there are 32 blocks in this pattern, this is a good project for a group of quilters to work on together, as each pieced block is identical. One person might do all cutting while others pin the pieces together for each block. It's easy to hand-quilt this patchwork by simply following the seam lines and then quilting all the squares with an X from corner to corner.

MATERIALS

All fabric is 45 inches wide.
1½ yards dark fabric A
3½ yards light fabric B
4 yards fabric for backing
quilt batting

DIRECTIONS

Cut the following:

From fabric A:
      15 strips, each 3½ × 42 inches

From fabric B:
      12 strips, each 3½ × 42 inches
      31 squares, each 9½ × 9½ inches

STRIP PIECING

Unit 1

1. Refer to Figure 1. With right sides facing and raw edges aligned, join 1 A strip to 1 B strip along one long edge, leaving a ¼-inch seam allowance.
2. Open seams and press.
3. Join another A strip to the B strip so you have one strip of light, dark, light fabric.
4. Cut this strip into 3½-inch segments as shown. There will be 12 segments.
5. Repeat Steps 1 through 4 until you have 64 segments, each 3½ inches wide.

Unit 2

1. Repeat Steps 1 through 5, reversing the fabric order. In other words, stitch a light B strip to a dark A strip, followed by another B strip.
2. Cut into 3½-inch segments. There will be 12 segments. Continue to do this until you have 32 segments, each 3½ inches wide.

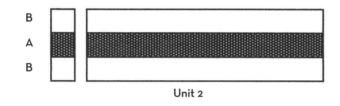

Unit 1

Unit 2

Figure 1. Strip piece Units 1 and 2.

TO MAKE A BLOCK

There are 32 pieced blocks in this quilt. Each block is 9 × 9 inches. Each pieced block is separated by a solid fabric block 9 × 9 inches, of which there are 31.

1. Refer to Figure 2. With right sides facing and raw edges aligned, stitch a Segment 1 to a Segment 2 along one long edge as shown. Open seams and press.
2. Repeat with a Segment 1 as shown. You have now completed one block. Make 32 of these blocks.

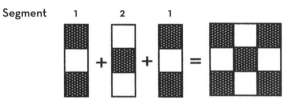

Figure 2. Make a 9-piece block.

TO MAKE ROWS

1. With right sides facing and raw edges aligned, join a pieced block with a solid block along one side edge as shown in Figure 3. Open seams and press.
2. Continue to join blocks in this way until you have a row of 4 pieced blocks separated by 3 solid blocks. Open and press seams.
3. Begin the next row with a solid block, followed by a pieced block, until you have joined 4 solid blocks divided by 3 pieced blocks as shown in Figure 4.
4. Alternate rows in this way until you have 9 rows of 7 blocks each.

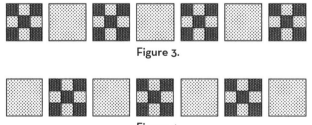

Figure 3.

Figure 4.

Figures 3 and 4. Join blocks. Make rows.

TO JOIN ROWS

1. Refer to Figure 5 to assemble, alternating rows. With right sides facing and raw edges aligned, pin Rows 1 and 2 together along one edge. Stitch together along one edge.
2. Open all seams and press.
3. Continue to join rows in this way as shown.

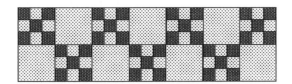

Figure 5. Join rows.

TO PREPARE BACKING

1. Cut the batting ¼ inch smaller than the quilt top all around.
2. Cut the 4 yards of backing fabric in half lengthwise so you have two pieces of 2 yards each.
3. With right sides facing and raw edges aligned, stitch these pieces together along one long edge. You now have a backing piece that measures 72 × 90 inches.
4. Trim the backing to the quilt top size.
5. Baste the top, batting, and backing together with long stitches through all 3 layers. Begin at the center of the quilt and baste to each outer corner. If necessary to keep fabric from slipping, baste around outside edges as well.

Irish Chain Quilt

TO QUILT

The quilting can be done on the machine if you want to finish the project quickly. Hand-stitching, however, makes the quilt look better and adds to the heirloom quality we admire in old quilts.

1. Begin at the center of the quilt to avoid bunching of the batting and work outward, taking small running stitches ¼ inch on either side of each seam line.
2. As you approach the outer edges of the quilt, stop stitching ½ inch before reaching the quilt edge so you have not stitched in the seam line. The raw edges will be turned under to finish the quilt.
3. To finish a line of quilting, pull the thread through to the backing side, make a small knot and pull back through the batting, popping the knot through the fabric. Clip the thread close to the quilt top. Or stitch over your last stitches several times to secure the end of the thread.

TO FINISH

1. When all quilting is complete, clip basting stitches away.
2. Fold all raw edges of the top under ¼ inch and press. Fold the backing edges to the inside and press. Stitch together with a slip stitch, blind stitch, or machine stitch.
3. If you want a slight trim of the backing fabric all around the quilt top, fold the top edges under ½ inch and press.
4. Next, bring the backing fabric forward and press ¼ inch all around. Fold again over the quilt top so there is a small (¼–½-inch) border all around. Stitch to the front of the quilt.
5. Bias tape is another way to finish the edge. Begin by trimming the edges of fabric top. Next, trim the backing to the same size as the top. Finish the edges by encasing them in double-sided matching or contrasting tape. See Figure 6 for the finished Irish Chain Quilt.

Figure 6. Finished Irish Chain Quilt.

4: AMISH SQUARE QUILT

Amish quilts are always among the most popular designs. The colors often include red, lavender, green, blue, and black, and the designs are simple and straightforward. Don't be put off by the 14 piecing steps, as this is one of the easiest quilts to make by basically adding squares, rectangles, and triangles to build one large square.

These quilts have a bold, graphic quality that is both traditional and contemporary in feeling. Use this quilt as a lap throw, a table cover, or a wall hanging. The finished size is 42 × 42 inches.

MATERIALS

All fabric is 45 inches wide.
¼ yard burgundy fabric
½ yard dusty lavender fabric
½ yard plum fabric
¾ yard bright blue fabric
1¾ yards black fabric
1½ yards quilt batting

DIRECTIONS

All measurements include a ¼-inch seam allowance.

Cut the following:

From burgundy:
 4 squares, each 3½ × 3½ inches
 4 squares, each 6 × 6 inches

From dusty lavender:
 1 square, 12½ × 12½ inches

From plum:

      2 squares, each 12⅞ × 12⅞ inches; cut each square across the diagonal to make
      2 triangles each (4 triangles)

From bright blue:

      4 strips, each 6 × 30½ inches
      4 squares, each 3 × 3 inches

From black:

      first, the backing piece, 45 × 45 inches
      4 strips, each 3 × 12½ inches
      4 strips, each 3½ × 24½ inches

TO MAKE THE QUILT TOP

1. Refer to Figure 1. With right sides facing and raw edges aligned, join a short black strip (3 × 12½ inches) to each side of the dusty lavender square. Press seams to one side.
2. Refer to Figure 2. With right sides facing and raw edges aligned, join a bright blue square to each short end of the remaining 2 shorter black strips to make 2 longer strips.
3. Refer to Figure 3. Pin one of these long strips to the top edge of the dusty lavender square and another strip to the bottom edge to make a larger square as shown in Figure 4. Stitch across each pinned edge.
4. Press seams to one side.

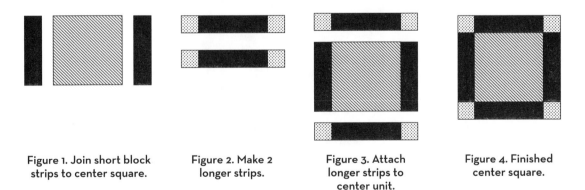

Figure 1. Join short block strips to center square.

Figure 2. Make 2 longer strips.

Figure 3. Attach longer strips to center unit.

Figure 4. Finished center square.

Figures 1 to 4. Center block.

5. Refer to Figure 5. With right sides facing and raw edges aligned, stitch the diago-

nal edge of a plum triangle to each side edge of this larger square.

6. Repeat on the top and bottom edges of this larger square.

7. Press seams to one side.

8. With right sides facing, join a black strip (3½ × 24½ inches) to each side of this square. Press seams to one side.

9. Refer to Figure 6. Stitch a small burgundy square to each short end of the remaining 2 black strips to make 2 longer strips.

10. Refer to Figure 7. With right sides facing, stitch one of these longer strips to the top edge and another to the bottom edge of the square,

11. Press seams to one side.

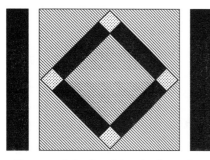

Figure 5. Join plum triangles to center block. Add a black strip to each side.

Figure 6. Make 2 longer strips.

Figure 7. Add a longer strip to top and bottom of unit to make the outer square.

Figures 5 to 7. Middle block.

12. With right sides facing and raw edges aligned, stitch a bright blue strip to each side of the square. Press seams to one side.

13. Refer to Figure 8. Join a large burgundy square to each short end of the remaining 2 bright blue strips to make 2 longer strips.

14. With right sides facing, stitch one of these longer strips to the top edge and another to the bottom edge to complete the quilt top as shown.

15. Press seams to one side.

Join a blue strip to each side of the outer square.
Make 2 longer strips from bright blue strips and burgundy
squares. Attach a longer strip to the top and bottom
of unit to make a large square.

Figure 8. Assembly.

Amish Square Quilt

TO QUILT

1. With wrong sides facing and batting between, pin backing, batting, and quilt top together.
2. Beginning at the center and working outward in a sunburst pattern, take long, loose basting stitches through all 3 layers.
3. Using small, running stitches, quilt on either sides of all seam lines.
4. Many Amish quilts have intricate quilt patterns over the entire fabric. Templates for these patterns are available in fabric stores or you can create your own pattern of evenly spaced, diagonal lines (see page 17). Follow these premarked lines with running stitches if desired.

TO FINISH

1. When all quilting is complete, remove the basting stitches.
2. Trim the batting to the same size as the quilt top.
3. Trim the backing fabric to 1 inch larger than the quilt top all around.
4. Turn the raw edges of the backing fabric forward ¼ inch and press.
5. Fold the remaining backing fabric over onto the quilt top to form a ½-inch black border all around the quilt as shown in Figure 9. Pin to the quilt top.
6. Slip-stitch or machine-stitch all around. See Figure 9 for the finished Amish Square.

TO HANG

There are many ways to hang a quilt. Since this wall hanging is small and lightweight, you have several options that are not practical for hanging a heavier, full-size quilt. Choose from the following what will work best for the area where the wall hanging will be placed:

1. Attach a small Velcro tab to the back of each corner of the quilt and another in the center of each side edge. Then attach the corresponding tabs to the wall and position the wall hanging firmly to the wall.
2. Sew a 2-inch strip of muslin to the backing across the top of the quilt to create a channel through which you can insert a dowel, a curtain rod, or a flat piece of wood.

The insert should be slightly longer than the quilt so that it can be suspended on brackets.

3. Attach a strip of Velcro to a wooden frame such as an artist's stretcher bar. Then attach corresponding Velcro strips to the back of the quilt and stretch it onto the frame. Hang it as you would a painting.

Figure 9. Finished Amish Square.

5: CHECKERBOARD QUILT

This is one of the easiest quilts to make because it consists of large patchwork squares sewn together in rows. A border of one of the fabrics is added all around. The interest comes from the use of fabric: a solid green with solid white and a stripe of green and white, to create a bold, two-color contemporary design. You can choose any two colors to go with your room to achieve the same effect. Use this pattern and the basic directions to make a smaller version for a crib quilt or add squares and a larger border all around to make it fit a queen- or king-size bed. This quilt is 64 × 88 inches, just right for a single bed.

This is the perfect project for 4 members of a quilting club to make together. There are 4 different fabrics from which to cut 24 squares each. Dividing this part of the process cuts the preparation work down to one-fourth. However, if you're making this quilt by yourself, it is easy to cut all the squares at once since each piece is identical.

MATERIALS

All fabric is 45 inches wide.
¾ yard light green fabric A
¾ yard white fabric B
2½ yards dark green fabric C
¾ yard green and white striped fabric D
3¾ yards backing fabric
quilt batting

DIRECTIONS

All measurements include a ¼-inch seam allowance.

Cut the following:

From light green A:
    24 squares, each 6½ × 6½ inches

From white B:
    24 squares, each 6½ × 6½ inches

From dark green C:
    Borders:
        2 strips, each 8½ × 48½ inches (top and bottom)
        2 strips, each 8½ × 88½ inches (sides)
    24 squares, each 6½ × 6½ inches

From striped fabric D:
    24 squares, each 6½ × 6½ inches

TO MAKE ROWS

Note: When joining squares to make up the rows, be sure to follow Figure 1 and Step 3 for placement of squares in each row, taking special care with the horizontal and vertical placement of the striped fabric. Also be sure seams are lined up under each other. These are the only precautions necessary for a successful project.

1. With right sides facing and raw edges aligned, join an A square to a B square along one side edge. Open seams and press.
2. Join a C square, then a D square, followed by an A, then B, then C, ending with a D square. Open all seams and press.
3. Refer to Figure 1. Continue to make rows following the sequence below. You will have a total of 12 rows of 8 squares each.

Quilting Club Tip:

If you are making this as a group, one person can pin a row together while another stitches them on the machine. If there are 4 of you, each person will pin 3 rows of squares together.

Row 2: B–C–D–A–B–C–D–A
Row 3: C–D–A–B–C–D–A–B
Row 4: D–A–B–C–D–A–B–C
Row 5: A–B–C–D–A–B–C–D
Row 6: B–C–D–A–B–C–D–A
Row 7: C–D–A–B–C–D–A–B
Row 8: D–A–B–C–D–A–B–C
Row 9: A–B–C–D–A–B–C–D
Row 10: B–C–D–A–B–C–D–A
Row 11: C–D–A–B–C–D–A–B
Row 12: D–A–B–C–D–A–B–C

4. Open all seams and press.

Figure 1. Add borders.

TO JOIN ROWS

1. With right sides facing and all seams aligned, pin Row 1 to Row 2 and stitch along the bottom edge. Open seams and press.
2. Continue to join rows in this way, making sure all seam lines match perfectly.

TO ADD BORDERS

1. With right sides facing and raw edges aligned, pin the 8½ × 48½-inch dark green top border strip to the top edge of the pieced quilt top.
2. Stitch together along the top edge. Open seam and press. Repeat on the bottom edge of the quilt.
3. Join the dark green 8½ × 88½-inch side borders in the same way.

TO PREPARE BACKING

1. Cut the fabric in half.
2. With right sides facing, stitch these 2 pieces together along one side edge.
3. Trim the backing about 2–3 inches larger than the quilt top all around.

TO QUILT

1. Pin the quilt top to the quilt batting and then to the backing fabric.
2. Starting at the center and working outward in a sunburst pattern, take long basting stitches through all 3 layers of fabric. The basting lines should be about 6 inches apart.
3. Hand stitching always looks best, but if you want to do this on the machine to save time, loosen the tension and set to about 6–8 stitches to the inch. Stitch along all seam lines on the quilt top. Stop stitching within ½ inch of the edges all around.
4. For hand quilting: Take small running stitches ¼ inch on each side of all seam lines through all 3 layers of fabric. Do not stitch into ½-inch seam allowance all around quilt.

Note: To make this project quickly, eliminate all quilting and machine-stitch around the inside and outside edges of the border to hold the 3 layers of fabric together.

TO FINISH

1. Clip away all basting stitches.
2. Turn raw edges of the backing and top fabrics ½ inch to the inside and press. Pin all around.
3. Machine-stitch around the quilt, close to the outside edge. See Figure 2 for finished Checkerboard Quilt.

Figure 2. Finished Checkerboard Quilt.

6: LOG CABIN MINI PILLOWS

The Log Cabin pattern is always attractive and easily adaptable for a project of any size. We've used this popular pattern to make small pillows with a red and white theme, as was often the choice of early quilters. You can fill the 8 × 8-inch pillows with cotton stuffing or with pine needles to add a fresh scent to a room The hand quilting gives them a special, old-fashioned look.

During the holidays, pile a few in a basket to display on a table. This is the perfect project to make for hostess gifts, or turn them into ornaments for your tree. Have the kids help and they can give a handmade Christmas ornament to their grandparents.

MATERIALS

All fabric is 45 inches wide.
¼ yard red solid
¼ yard white solid
1 yard premade piping for each pillow
stuffing
quilt batting (8-inch square for each pillow)
tracing paper
cardboard or acetate

DIRECTIONS

All measurements include a ¼-inch seam allowance.

1. Trace the square pattern templates (page 60) and transfer to cardboard.
2. Cut the following for 3 pillows:

   From red:
   > 2 backing pieces, each 8½ × 8½ inches
   > 1 square, 2½ × 2½ inches
   > 1 square, 1½ × 1½ inches
   > from remaining fabric, cut 1½-inch-wide strips

From white:

    1 backing piece, 8½ × 8½ inches

    1 square, 2½ × 2½ inches

    1 square, 1½ × 1½ inches

    from remaining fabric, cut 1½-inch-wide strips

Pillow 1

1. Refer to Figure 1. With right sides facing, stitch a red strip to one side of the 2½ × 2½-inch square as shown. Cut off the remainder of the red strip. Press seams to one side.

2. Refer to Figure 2. Stitch the red strip to the opposite side of the white square. Cut off the remainder of the strip as shown. Press seams to one side.

3. Refer to Figure 3. With right sides facing, join a white strip to the top edge of this unit. Cut off the remainder of the white strip and stitch it to the bottom edge of this unit.

4. Refer to Figure 4. Continue adding a red strip to each side and a white strip to the top and bottom edges 2 more times. Press seams to one side.

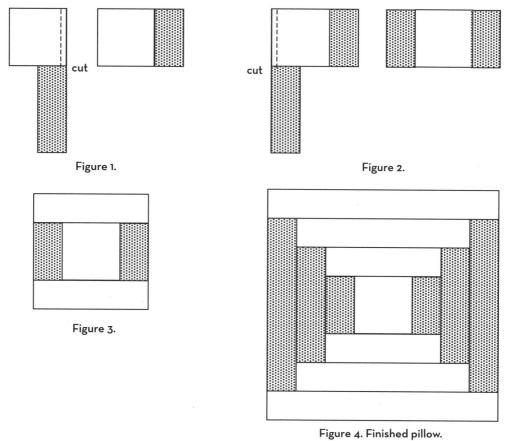

Figure 1.

Figure 2.

Figure 3.

Figure 4. Finished pillow.

Figures 1 to 4. Pillow 1.

Pillow 2

1. Refer to Figure 5. With right side facing, stitch a white strip to the top edge of the red 2½ × 2½-inch square as shown. Cut off the remainder of the white strip. Press seams to one side.
2. Refer to Figure 6. Stitch the white strip to the right side of the red square as shown. Cut off the remainder of the strip. Press seams to one side.
3. Refer to Figure 7. With right sides facing, stitch a red strip to the bottom edge of this unit. Cut off the remainder of the red strip and stitch this to the left side of the unit as shown. Press seams to one side.
4. Refer to Figure 8. Attach a white strip to the top and one to the right side of the unit, then a red strip to the bottom and another to the left side of the unit 2 more times as shown. Press seams to one side.

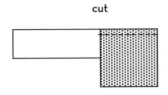

cut

Figure 5.

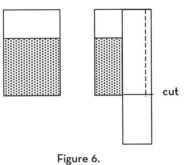

cut

Figure 6.

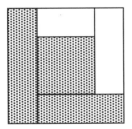

Figure 7.

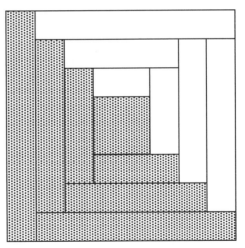

Figure 8. Finished pillow.

Figures 5 to 8. Pillow 2.

Log Cabin Mini Pillows

Pillow 3

1. Refer to Figure 9. With right sides facing, stitch the white 1½ × 1½-inch square to the red square of the same size along one side edge as shown.
2. Refer to Figure 10. Stitch a red strip to the top edge of this unit as shown. Cut off the remainder of the red strip. Press seams to one side.
3. Refer to Figure 11. With right sides facing, stitch a white strip to the left side of this unit. Cut off the remainder of the white strip and stitch to the bottom edge of the unit as shown. Press seams to one side.
4. Refer to Figure 12. Stitch a red strip to the right side of the unit. Cut off the remainder of the strip and join to the top of the unit as shown. Join a white strip to the left side and another white strip to the bottom edge of the unit, then a red strip to the right side and another to the top edge 2 more times as shown. Press seams to one side.

Note: To make these pillow larger, continue the pattern by adding strips to each side in the same way.

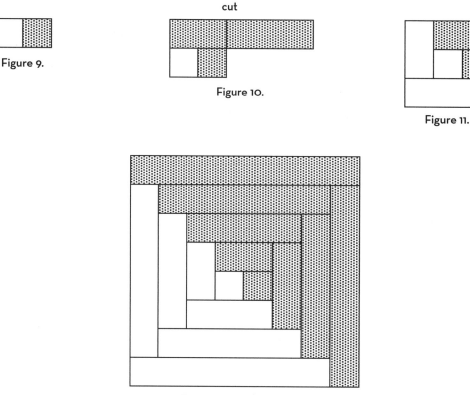

Figure 9.

cut

Figure 10.

Figure 11.

Figure 12. Finished pillow.

Figures 9 to 12. Pillow 3.

TO QUILT

1. Pin each pillow top to a piece of batting slightly larger than the top.
2. Using small running stitches, quilt ⅛ inch on each side of all seam lines.

Tip:

Most quilting stitches on large projects are ¼ inch on each side of the seam lines, but when your strips are quite narrow and the project is small like this one, the quilting looks better closer to the seam lines.

TO FINISH

1. When all quilting has been completed, remove the pins and trim the batting ½ inch smaller than the pillow tops all around.
2. With right sides facing and raw edges aligned, pin the piping to the pillow tops, overlapping where the ends meet.
3. Using the zipper foot on your sewing machine, stitch close to the piping all around.
4. With right sides facing, pin a backing piece to each pillow top. Using the piping stitches as your guide, stitch around 3 sides and 4 corners.
5. Clip the corners, turn right side out, and stuff. Turn the raw edges of the opening to the inside and slip-stitch closed.

1½-inch pattern

2½-inch pattern

Pattern Templates.

7: COLORFUL BABY BLOCKS QUILT

Create a cheerful crib quilt with ice cream–colored squares divided by lattice strips of white. This is an easy project to make and fun to give. The finished size is 40 inches × 46 inches and will fit a standard crib. To make this in a group, give each person a task with one member marking the squares on the fabric while another cuts them out. Another person can pin squares together to create the rows while another is stitching them together. It will take one evening to piece the entire quilt top.

MATERIALS

All fabric is 45 inches wide.
1½ yards yellow gingham
1½ yards backing fabric
¾ yard white
⅛ yard each: cream A, blue B, light green C, pink D, yellow E solids
cotton quilt batting 40 × 46 inches
tracing paper
cardboard or acetate

DIRECTIONS

All measurements include ¼-inch seam allowance.

1. Trace the square pattern (Figure 1) and transfer to cardboard to make a template. Seam allowance is included.
2. Cut the following:

   From yellow gingham:
       2 strips, each 4½ × 46½ inches (side borders)
       2 strips, each 4½ × 32½ inches (top and bottom borders)

Figure 1. Pattern.

From backing fabric:
1 piece, 41 × 47 inches

From white:
24 lattice strips, each 2½ × 4½ inches
7 lattice strips, each 2½ × 28½ inches
2 lattice strips, each 2½ × 38½ inches

From cream A, blue B, light green C, pink D, and yellow E solids:
6 squares each using pattern

TO MAKE A ROW

1. Refer to Figure 2. With right sides facing, stitch a 2½ × 4½-inch lattice strip to the right side of a cream A square.
2. Refer to Figure 3. Join a blue B square in the same way. Continue with another lattice strip same size, a green C square, another short lattice strip, a pink D square, another lattice strip, and end with a yellow E square to make a row of 5 squares separated by 4 lattice strips.
3. Follow the color sequence to make 5 more rows in the same way.

Figure 2. Join square to lattice strip.

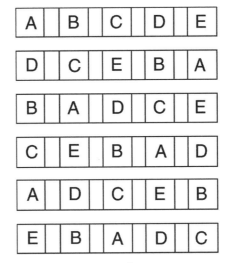

Figure 3. Make rows.

Figures 2 and 3.

Colorful Baby Blocks Quilt

TO JOIN ROWS

1. Refer to Figure 4. With right sides facing, stitch a 2½ × 28½-inch white lattice strip to the top edge of Row 1. Press seams to one side.
2. Join another lattice strip of the same size to the bottom edge of Row 1. Continue to join all 6 rows separated by 2½ × 28½-inch white lattice strips in this way, ending with a lattice strip along the bottom edge as shown.
3. With right sides facing and raw edges aligned, join a 2½ × 38½-inch white lattice strip to each side of the joined rows. Press seams to one side.

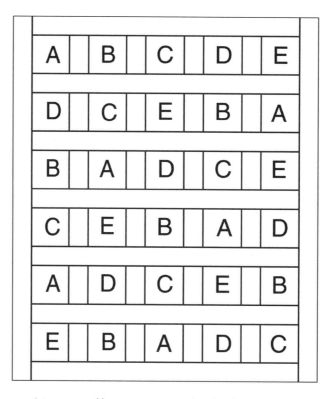

Join rows and lattice strip to each side of joined rows.

Figure 4. Assembly.

TO MAKE BORDERS

1. Refer to Figure 5. With right sides facing and raw edges aligned, pin a 4½ × 32½-inch yellow gingham border strip to the top edge of the quilt. Stitch across. Repeat on the bottom edge of the quilt. Press seams to one side.
2. Join remaining yellow gingham strips to side edges in the same way. Press seams to one side.

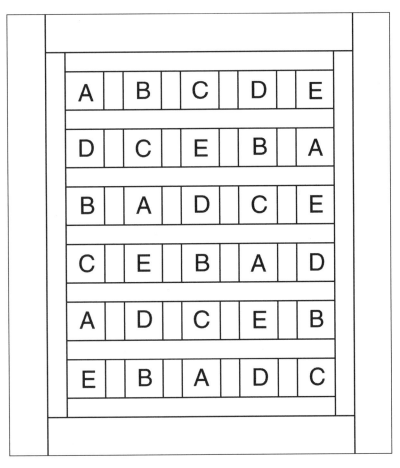

Add borders to make the finished Colorful Baby Blocks Quilt.

Figure 5. Assembly.

Colorful Baby Blocks Quilt

TO QUILT

1. Center the batting on the wrong side of the backing fabric. Place quilt top right side up on batting and pin all 3 layers together.
2. Beginning at the center of the quilt and working outward, baste all 3 layers together with long, loose stitches in a sunburst pattern.
3. To quilt by hand: Take small running stitches on each side of all seam lines through all 3 layers.
4. To machine-quilt: Stitch in the channel of all seam lines.
5. For either hand or machine quilting: Stop stitches ½ inch from the edge of the quilt all around. Do not stitch into the outside seam allowance
6. Remove basting stitches. Trim the batting ½ inch smaller than the quilt top all around. Trim the backing to the same size as the quilt top.

TO FINISH

1. Turn the raw edges of the quilt top and backing to the inside ¼ inch and press.
2. Slip-stitch or machine-stitch all around to close.

Shoo-Fly Quilt (page 24)

Irish Chain Quilt (page 38)

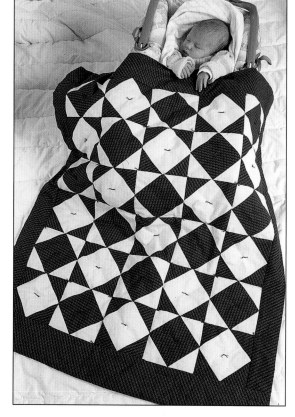

Baby's First Quilt (page 32)

Amish Square Quilt (page 44)

Checkerboard Quilt (page 50)

Log Cabin Mini Pillows (page 55)

Colorful Baby Blocks Quilt (page 61)

Flowers and Bows Lap Throw (page 67)

Pinwheel Crib Quilt (page 72)

Pinwheel Pillows (page 81)

Rose Coverlet (page 87)

Around-the-World Quilt (page 92)

8: FLOWERS AND BOWS LAP THROW

Nothing is easier to make than a small quilt with pieced squares. If you've made new curtains, a bedspread, or even a piece of clothing, chances are you have left over remnants, or a few inches of the full width of the fabric in different prints or colors. These strips may be too small to make anything other than a sachet or potholder, but they can be cut into squares of equal size and used to make a pretty lap throw. If you don't have scraps of fabric, choose a combination of pretty floral prints and buy small amounts. Fabric shops always have remnants of decorator fabric on sale. Another design idea is to cut up pieces of fabric in the colors of your school or sorority.

The trick to making this project look good is the selection and combination of fabrics and colors. This throw was made from floral-printed, pastel-colored fabrics left over from other home accessories in the same room. It measures 40 × 48 inches. (See color photo.)

MATERIALS

All fabric is 45 inches wide. You will need a small amount of 8 different fabrics that look good together in the following amounts:

⅛ yard fabric A
⅛ yard fabric B
1½ yards fabric C (includes borders)
¼ yard D
¼ yard E
⅛ yard F
⅛ yard G
⅛ yard H
1½ yards backing fabric
quilt batting 40 × 47 inches
tracing paper
cardboard or acetate

DIRECTIONS

All measurements include a ¼-inch seam allowance.

1. Trace the pattern (Figure 1) and transfer to cardboard to make a template. Seam allowance is included.
2. Cut 6 squares from A.
3. Cut 4 squares from B.
4. Cut borders, as follows, then cut squares from C:
   2 strips, each 4 × 39½ inches (top and bottom)
   2 strips, each 4 × 47½ inches (sides)
5. Cut 18 squares from D.
6. Cut 16 squares from E.
7. Cut 8 squares from F.
8. Cut 8 squares from G.
9. Cut 4 squares from H.

TO MAKE ROWS

1. Refer to Figure 2. With right sides facing, join an F square and a B square along the right side edge. Press seams to one side.
2. With right sides facing, join an E square to the opposite side edge of the B square. Press seams to one side.
3. Continue to join an H square, then an A square, followed by a D square, then a C square, and ending Row 1 with an E square.
4. Press seams to one side.
5. Refer to Figure 2 for the color sequence and make 10 rows of 9 squares in this way.

TO JOIN ROWS

1. Refer again to Figure 2. With right sides facing and seams aligned, join the bottom long edge of Row 1 to the top long edge of Row 2. Press seams to one side.
2. Continue to join rows in this way in the sequence shown.

Figure 1. Pattern.

Flowers and Bows Lap Throw

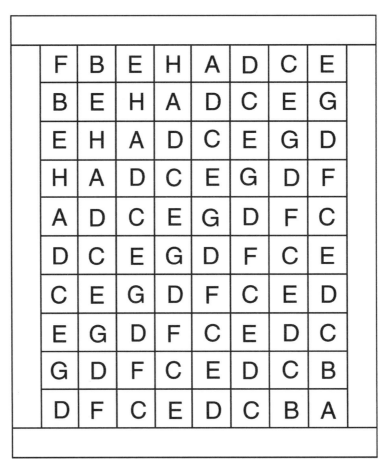

**Join rows and add borders to make the finished
Flowers and Bows Lap Throw.**

Figure 2. Assembly.

TO JOIN BORDERS

1. With right sides facing, join a side border strip to one side edge of the quilt top.
2. Press seams to one side.
3. Repeat on the opposite side edge of the quilt in the same way.
4. With right sides facing, join one of the remaining border strips to the top edge of the quilt. Press seams to one side.
5. Repeat with the bottom border strip in the same way.

TO QUILT

1. Cut the backing fabric 41½ × 49½ inches.
2. With wrong sides facing and batting between, pin backing fabric, batting, and patchwork top together. There will be 1½ inches of extra backing fabric all around.
3. Beginning at the center and working outward in a sunburst pattern, take long, loose, basting stitches through all 3 layers.
4. Using small, running stitches, quilt ¼ inch on each side of all seam lines, stopping short of the seam allowance all around the outside edge of the quilt.

TO FINISH

1. When all quilting is complete, remove basting stitches.
2. Trim batting to same size as quilt top.
3. Fold ¼ inch of backing fabric forward and press.
4. Bring the remaining backing fabric forward to encase the raw edges of the quilt and create a 1-inch border around the top of the quilt.
5. Press and slip-stitch all around to finish.

9: PINWHEEL CRIB QUILT

This quilt pattern takes its name from a child's pinwheel design, a familiar motif in American folk quilts. It is frequently made with red and white triangles for a bold playful effect. This time I thought it would be nice to make it soft and cuddly by using pastels. Consider flannel fabric for this quilt.

The technique employs the quick and easy triangle method, which makes it very easy to piece together. Only one template is used to make the blocks. The borders frame the center design and enable you to adjust the size. The finished quilt size is 37×54 inches. This quilt is inexpensive to make because it takes under 4 yards of fabric.

MATERIALS

All fabric is 45 inches wide.
½ yard light green printed fabric
½ yard light blue printed fabric
¾ yard yellow fabric
2 yards peach fabric (includes backing)
1½ yards quilt batting
tracing paper
cardboard or acetate

Quilting Club Tip:

If you are making this quilt in a group, make one pattern piece (Figure 1) for each color fabric and have each quilter cut the number of pieces needed from one color fabric each. For example: One person cuts 12 blue squares, another cuts 12 green squares, and two people cut 12 squares each from yellow. Someone else can be responsible for cutting all peach strips. This will save cutting time.

DIRECTIONS

1. Trace the pattern (Figure 1) to make a template. This pattern represents half the piece needed. A ¼-inch seam allowance is included.

2. Fold the fabric in half so you have a double layer and pin the pattern on the fold of the fabric where indicated on the template. Cut out to make one large triangle shape. Use the pattern to cut the following:

   12 pieces from light blue

   12 pieces from light green

   24 pieces from yellow

3. Cut backing, lattice, and border strips from peach:

   backing piece, 37½ × 54½ inches

   2 border strips, each 3½ × 54½ inches (sides)

   4 lattice strips, each 3½ × 31½ inches

   3 lattice strips, each 3½ × 14½ inches

4. Cut a piece of batting 35½ × 51½ inches.

Pinwheel Crib Quilt

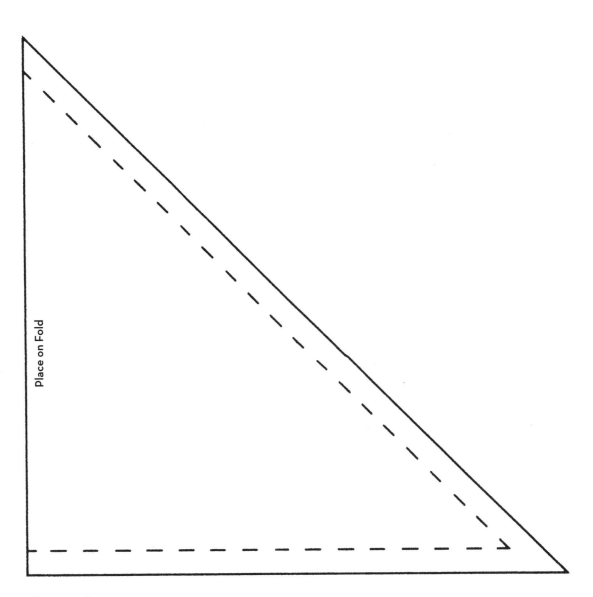

Place on Fold

Figure 1. Pattern.

TO MAKE A BLOCK

1. Refer to Figure 2. With right sides facing and raw edges aligned, join a yellow triangle piece with a matching blue triangle along the diagonal to make a square. Open seams and press. Make 3 more squares in this way.
2. Refer to Figure 3. Repeat 3 more times to make 4 squares.
3. With right sides facing and raw edges aligned, join squares along right side edge. Open seams and press.
4. Join two more squares in the same way.
5. Refer to Figure 4. With right sides facing and seams aligned, join top 2 squares to bottom 2 squares to make a block.
6. Make 3 blocks using the yellow and blue triangles and 3 blocks using the green and yellow triangles.

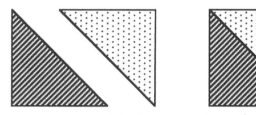

Figure 2. Join triangles to make square.

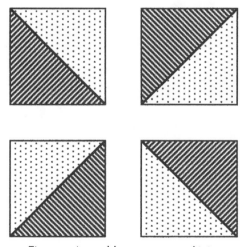

Figure 3. Assemble 4 squares and join.

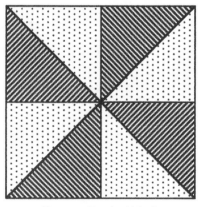

Figure 4. Finished block.

Figures 2 to 4. Make a block.

TO JOIN BLOCKS

1. Refer to Figure 5. With right sides facing and raw edges aligned, stitch one short peach lattice strip (3½ × 14½ inches) to the right side edge of a blue block. Press seams to one side.
2. Join this to the left side of a green block to make the top row of the quilt. Press seams to one side.
3. Alternate the blue and green blocks to make the middle and bottom rows in the same way. Press seams to one side.
4. Refer to Figure 6. With right sides facing and raw edges aligned, pin one of the 4 long peach lattice strips (3½ × 31½ inches) to the top edge of the top row of blocks. Stitch across, open seams, and press.
5. With right sides facing, join a peach lattice strip to the bottom of the top row, followed by the middle row, a peach lattice strip, the bottom row, and a peach lattice strip. Press all seams to one side.
6. Refer to Figure 7. With right sides facing and raw edges aligned, attach the 2 long peach border strips, 3½ × 54½ inches, to each side of the quilt top in the same way.

Figure 5. Join blocks to make a row.

Figure 6. Join rows.

Pinwheel Crib Quilt

Figure 7. Add border strips.

TO QUILT

1. With wrong sides facing, pin the top of the quilt, the batting, and backing fabric together.
2. Begin at the center of the quilt and take long, loose basting stitches outward in a sunburst pattern through all 3 layers.
3. Using small running stitches, quilt ¼ inch from each side of all seam lines. Stop quilting stitches ½ inch from outer edges all around.

TO FINISH

1. Remove basting stitches.
2. Trim batting ½ inch smaller than quilt top all around. Trim backing to the same size as the quilt top.
3. Turn the raw edges of the quilt top and backing to the inside ¼ inch all around and press.
4. Pin together and slip-stitch or machine-stitch close to the edge all around. Press. See Figure 8 for the finished Pinwheel Quilt.

> **Quilting Club Tip:**
>
> This is an excellent project for 3 or 6 people to work on together to make a baby gift from all of you. Depending on how many people are in the group, each person will make one or two blocks to create the patchwork top. Each person can then hand-quilt only one or two blocks before putting them together with the lattice strip.

Figure 8. Finished Pinwheel Quilt.

10: PINWHEEL PILLOWS

The pinwheel pillows are perfect small quilting projects. While they go with the pinwheel quilt, each uses a slightly different color combination of the same fabrics. The finished size is 12 × 12 inches and can be filled with stuffing or a standard pillow form. This is a good first project and makes a lovely baby gift. If you've formed a quilting club, each person might make their own pillow using the same pattern but with different fabrics.

MATERIALS

(For 2 pillows)
½ yard peach fabric
½ yard blue fabric
⅓ yard green fabric
⅓ yard yellow fabric
½ yard quilt batting
12 × 12-inch pillow forms or stuffing
49 inches cording for each pillow
tracing paper
cardboard or acetate

DIRECTIONS

All measurements include a ¼-inch seam allowance.

Trace Patterns A and B (Figure 1) and transfer to cardboard to make templates. Seam allowance is included.

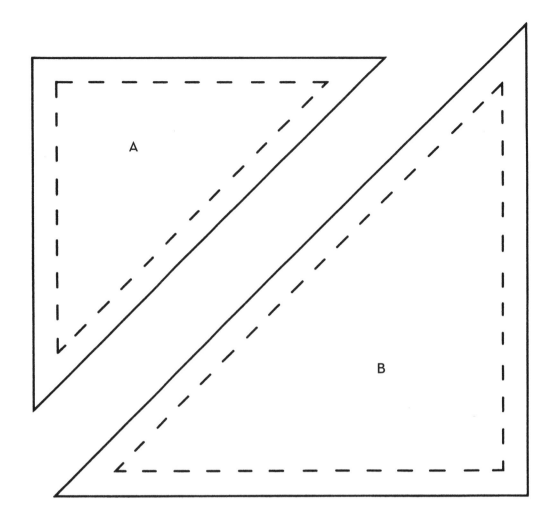

Figure 1. Patterns A and B.

Pillow 1

Cut the following:

From green:
    4 triangles using Pattern A

From yellow:
    2 strips, each 1½ × 10½ inches
    2 strips, each 1½ × 12½ inches
    4 triangles using Pattern B

From peach:
    backing piece, 12½ × 12½ inches
    4 triangles using Pattern B

TO ASSEMBLE

1. Refer to Figure 2. With right sides facing and raw edges aligned, join a yellow B triangle to a peach B triangle along one edge to make a large triangle as shown.
2. Press seams to one side.
3. Repeat with the remaining yellow B and peach B triangles.
4. With right sides facing and long edges aligned, join all yellow-peach triangles to each green A triangle. Press seams to one side.

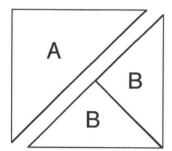 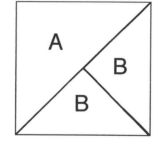 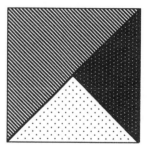

Figure 2. Join triangles to make a square.

5. Refer to Figure 3. Join all 4 squares, making a small pinwheel in the center of the pillow top. Press seams to one side.

6. Refer to Figure 4. Add the borders in the following way: With right sides facing and raw edges aligned, attach a short $1\frac{1}{2} \times 10\frac{1}{2}$-inch strip to one side edge of the block. Press seams to one side. Repeat on the opposite side.

7. Refer to Figure 5. Join the long strips to the top and bottom edge in the same way to complete the pillow top.

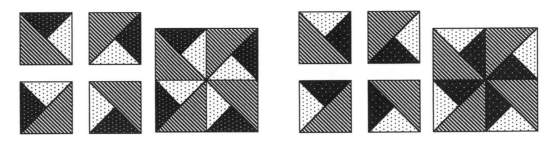

Figure 3. Assemble pillow tops.

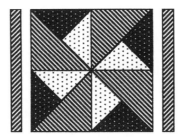

Figure 4.

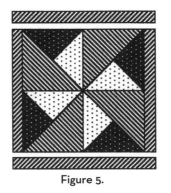

Figure 5.

Figures 4 and 5. Add borders.

TO QUILT

1. Cut the quilt batting 11½ × 11½ inches and pin to the back of the pillow top.
2. Taking small, running stitches, quilt ¼ inch on each side of all seam lines.

TO FINISH

It is not necessary to add piping around the edge of the pillow, but it adds a nice finishing touch. If you don't add piping, skip to Step 6.

1. Use any one of the fabrics to make a strip 1½ × 50 inches long for the piping to go around the pillow top. To do this, cut shorter strips of fabric on the bias and stitch the short ends of each strip together to make one long strip.
2. Beginning ½ inch from the end of the fabric, place the cording in the center of the wrong side of the fabric. Fold the fabric over the cording so the raw edges of the fabric meet.
3. Using the zipper foot on your sewing machine, stitch as close to the cording as possible to encase it in the fabric.
4. With right sides facing and raw edges aligned, pin the piping around the edge of the pillow top, overlapping the ends.
5. Stitch the piping to the pillow top as close to the cording as possible.
6. With right sides facing and raw edges aligned, stitch the backing piece to the pillow top, using the piping stitches as a guide and leave 8 inches across one edge open for turning. Trim seams and clip corners.
7. Turn right side out and insert pillow form or stuffing. Slip-stitch opening closed or insert a zipper according to package directions.

Pinwheel Pillows

Pillow 2

Cut the following:

From blue:
    backing piece 12½ × 12½ inches
    4 triangles using Pattern A

From yellow:
    4 triangles using Pattern B

From peach:
    2 strips, each 1½ × 10½ inches
    2 strips, each 1½ × 12½ inches
    4 triangles using Pattern B

DIRECTIONS

Follow directions for making Pillow 1.

Pillow 1

Pillow 2

Figure 6. Finished Pinwheel Pillows.

11: ROSE COVERLET

You will find remnants of decorator fabrics such as floral polished cotton at most fabric outlets. Look for a large print that can be cut into squares for a lovely patchwork coverlet. When I had new slipcovers made for my living room, I had leftover fabric that was perfect for a matching coverlet to drape over the sofa. The finished size is 51 inches square. Each 14-inch square is separated with green lattice strips. The coverlet is perfect as a lap throw, wall hanging, or table covering. It is good-looking and a cinch to make. While I've figured the yardage for 45-inch-wide fabric, most decorator fabrics are 52 or 54 inches wide so you may not need as much material as indicated below. Take this into consideration when buying fabric.

MATERIALS

1¼ yards printed fabric
1½ yards dark green fabric (or other solid to go with your print)
1½ yards 52-inch-wide fabric for backing
thin quilt batting

DIRECTIONS

All measurements include a ¼-inch seam allowance.

Cut the following:

From print:
    9 squares, each 14 × 14 inches, with motif centered on the squares

From green (or solid fabric):
    2 strips, each 3¼ × 52 inches (side borders)
    2 strips, each 3¼ × 46-½ inches (long lattice strips)
    6 strips, each 3¼ × 14 inches (short lattice strips)

Rose Coverlet

TO MAKE A ROW

1. Refer to Figure 1. With right sides facing and raw edges aligned, join a short lattice strip to the right side edge of a print square. Open seams and press.
2. Continue by adding another square, then a short lattice strip, then another print square to end the row as shown. This completes one row of squares in the 9-square coverlet. Open seams and press.
3. Make 3 rows in this way.

Figure 1. Make a row.

TO JOIN ROWS

1. Refer to Figure 2. With right sides facing and raw edges aligned, stitch a long green lattice strip to the top long edge of a row. Open seams and press.
2. Continue to add lattice strips and rows alternately, right sides facing, ending with a fourth lattice strip as shown. Open seams and press.
3. With right sides facing and raw edges aligned, stitch side border strips to the patchwork top. Open seams and press.

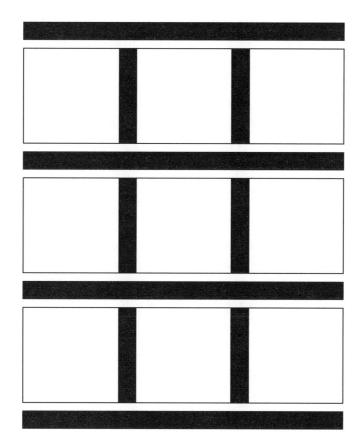

Figure 2. Join rows.

TO QUILT

1. Cut the batting ½ inch smaller than the top all around.
2. If you are using 52-inch-wide fabric for the backing, you do not need to seam the backing. If your fabric is 45 inches wide, you need to add a strip of fabric, 7 × 52 inches to one side edge.
3. With wrong sides facing, pin the top piece to the backing with the batting between. Secure the 3 layers of fabric together by tacking here and there in the seam lines

Rose Coverlet

where the squares and lattice strips meet. If you want to quilt the entire top, begin at the center and work outward, basting the top, batting, and backing together with long stitches through all 3 layers.

4. For quick quilting, machine-stitch along seam lines of each square and lattice strip. To hand-quilt, take small running stitches ¼ inch on both sides of the seam lines. Do not stitch into the seam allowance around the outer edges.

5. When all quilting is complete, clip away basting stitches.

TO FINISH

1. If you have not done any quilting, simply pin the backing to the top piece with right sides together. Stitch around all sides, leaving a few inches open for turning. Turn right side out, press, and slip-stitch opening closed.

2. Once you've quilted the entire top, fold the raw edges of the front under ¼ inch and press. Turn backing edges to the inside ¼ inch and press.

3. Stitch together with a slip stitch or machine stitch all around. See Figure 3 for the finished Rose Coverlet.

TO HANG

Sew a strip of Velcro to the top and bottom back edges. Measure carefully; apply a corresponding strip to the wall and press in position.

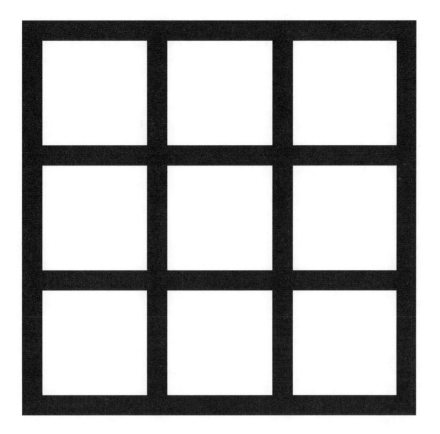

Figure 3. Finished Rose Coverlet.

12: AROUND-THE-WORLD QUILT

The basic colors—blue, green, yellow, and red—give this popular quilt pattern its vitality. It is a square patchwork 40 × 40 inches and makes a nice wall hanging. By selecting white, red, and green prints and solids, it becomes a wonderful holiday decoration. Choose any color combination to go with your décor. You can enlarge the finished size by adding an 8- to 10-inch border all around.

MATERIALS

All fabric is 45 inches wide.
2 yards blue fabric A (includes backing)
¾ yard red fabric B
¼ yard green fabric C
¼ yard yellow fabric D
1¼ yards thin quilt batting
Velcro tabs for hanging
tracing paper
cardboard or acetate

DIRECTIONS

All measurements include a ¼-inch seam allowance.

1. Trace the pattern (Figure 1) and transfer to cardboard to make a template. Seam allowance is included.
2. Cut the following:

   From blue A:
       backing piece, 41 × 41 inches
       48 squares, 3 × 3 inches (using the pattern in Figure 1)

Figure 1. Pattern.

From red B:

    24 squares, each 3 × 3 inches

    2 squares, each 20¼ × 20¼ inches, both cut into 2 triangles (total of 4 triangles)

From green C:

    24 squares, each 3 × 3 inches

From yellow D:

    25 squares, each 3 × 3 inches

TO MAKE ROWS

1. With right sides facing and raw edges aligned, stitch the squares together in the following sequence to make 11 rows:

A–A–B–C–D–A–D–C–B–A–A
A–B–C–D–A–A–A–D–C–B–A
B–C–D–A–A–B–A–A–D–C–B
C–D–A–A–B–C–B–A–A–D–C
D–A–A–B–C–D–C–B–A–A–D
A–A–B–C–D–D–D–C–B–A–A
D–A–A–B–C–D–C–B–A–A–D
C–D–A–A–B–C–B–A–A–D–C
B–C–D–A–A–B–A–A–D–C–B
A–B–C–D–A–A–A–D–C–B–A
A–A–B–C–D–A–D–C–B–A–A

2. Open all seams and press.

TO JOIN ROWS

1. Making sure that all seams line up, with right sides facing and raw edges aligned, join the first two rows along the bottom, long edge.
2. Open seams and press.
3. Continue to join rows in the sequence above.

TO FINISH TOP

1. With right sides facing and raw edges aligned, stitch the long edge of a red triangle to one side edge of the pieced squares. Open seams and press.
2. Continue to join the other 3 triangles in the same way.

TO QUILT

1. Place the top fabric on the batting and then the backing fabric and pin all 3 layers together.
2. Starting in the center and working outward in a sunburst pattern, take long basting stitches through the fabrics.
3. Using small running stitches, quilt ¼ inch on each side of all seam lines. Do not quilt into the seam allowance around the outside edges of the quilt.
4. If you want to add quilting stitches to the outside triangle pieces, you can do so by marking a grid with a yardstick (see page 17) and quilting along these lines. Or you can use a quilting template to make a pattern in each triangle and quilt in the same way.

TO FINISH

1. Remove all basting stitches.
2. Trim the batting so it is the same size as the quilt top.
3. Fold the edges of the backing under to the wrong side ¼ inch and press.
4. Fold the remaining edges of the backing fabric over onto the quilt top to create a border all around and pin in place. Press.
5. Slip-stitch or machine-stitch all around. See Figure 2 for the finished Around-the-World Quilt.

Figure 2. Finished Around-the-World Quilt.

13: CRAYON TRIANGLES FOR BABY

A crib-sized quilt is always a pleasure to make. It's manageable and easy to quilt in your lap. Many experienced quilters who have made quite elaborate quilt patterns are enjoying the experience of making small quilts. These projects can be completed quickly and make the most wonderful gifts. No matter how many times you wash a baby quilt, it gets softer and softer and looks better and better. This one is 32 × 44 inches and can be used as a wall hanging as well as a crib quilt. We used thin quilt batting, but if you prefer a puffier quilt, use a traditional loft.

This is an ideal quilt for using the quick and easy triangle method for cutting and stitching the two-color squares (see page 19). This is a good first project for a quilting club. Each member can use the same pattern with different colors, if desired.

MATERIALS

All fabric is 45 inches wide.
¼ yard solid blue
¼ yard solid raspberry
¼ yard solid purple
¼ yard solid pink
¼ yard solid yellow
¼ yard solid green
½ yard white
½ yard light green calico for borders
1 yard backing fabric
1 yard quilt batting
tracing paper
cardboard or acetate

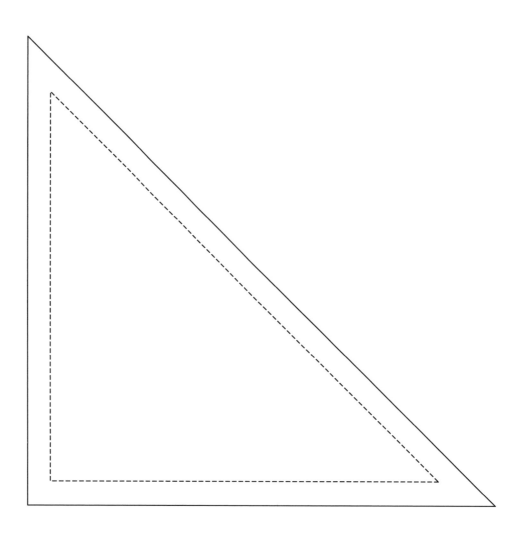

Figure 1. Pattern.

DIRECTIONS

All measurements include a ¼-inch seam allowance.

1. Trace the triangle pattern (Figure 1) and transfer to cardboard to make a template. Seam allowance is included.
2. Cut 9 triangles from each of the following colors: blue, raspberry, purple, pink, yellow, and green.
3. Cut 54 white triangles.
4. From light green calico, cut:
   2 border strips, each 4½ × 36½ inches (sides)
   2 border strips, each 4½ × 32½ inches (top and bottom)

TO MAKE SQUARES

1. Refer to Figure 2. With right sides facing, stitch a blue triangle to a white triangle along the diagonal to make a square.
2. Press seams to the blue side. Make 9 squares in this way.
3. Continue to join colored triangles to white triangles in this way to make 9 squares of each color with white for a total of 54 squares.
4. Press seams to color side.

Figure 2. Make a square.

Crayon Triangles for Baby

TO MAKE BLOCKS

Note: Each block uses 9 squares of the same color.

1. Refer to Figure 3. With right sides facing, and raw edges aligned, stitch 2 squares together along one side edge. Continue with another square to make a row of 3 squares.
2. Make 3 rows of 3 squares each in this way. Press all seams to the dark side.
3. With right sides facing, and raw edges aligned, pin the bottom edge of Row 1 to the top edge of Row 2 and stitch across. Press seams to the dark side.
4. Join the bottom edge of Row 2 to the top edge of Row 3 in the same way to make a block. Press seams to dark side.
5. Make one block of each color for a total of 6 blocks as shown in Figure 3.

Figure 3. Make blocks.

TO MAKE PATCHWORK QUILT TOP

1. With right sides facing and seams matching, pin and stitch the blue-white block to the raspberry-white block along one side edge. Press seams to the dark side. This is the top row of the quilt as shown.
2. Join the purple-white block to the pink-white block in the same way for the center row.
3. Join the yellow-white block to the green-white block for the bottom row of the quilt.
4. With right sides facing and seams matching, pin the bottom edge of Row 1 to the top edge of Row 2 and stitch across. Press seams to one side.
5. Repeat with Row 3 to complete the patchwork quilt top.

TO ADD BORDERS

1. Refer to Figure 4. With right sides facing, and raw edges aligned, pin a short border strip to each side of the quilt top and stitch.
2. Attach remaining border strips to the top and bottom edges of the quilt in the same way. Press seams to one side.

TO QUILT

If you want to have a quilting pattern in the borders as shown here, you will either use a quilting template (available in fabric shops) and trace the pattern onto the border fabric, or use a yardstick to mark a diagonal grid across the borders (see page 17). You may also leave the borders free of quilting for a simpler project.

1. With wrong sides facing, pin quilt top, batting, and backing together.
2. Beginning at the center of the quilt and working to the outer edges, take long, loose basting stitches through all 3 layers in a sunburst pattern.
3. Using small running stitches, quilt ¼ inch on each side of all seam lines in the blocks and along all premarked quilting lines in the borders, stopping ½ inch from the edges all around the quilt.

Crayon Triangles for Baby

Finished Crayon Triangles for Baby Quilt.

Figure 4. Assembly.

TO FINISH

1. When all quilting is complete, remove basting stitches.
2. Trim the batting to ½ inch smaller than the quilt top all around.
3. Trim the backing fabric to the same size as the quilt top.
4. Turn the raw edges of the quilt top and backing fabric to the inside ¼ inch on each side and press.
5. Pin together and then machine- or slip-stitch all around to close.

14: PATCHWORK TOTE

This is the perfect project to make with all those little leftover scraps of fabric from other projects. A tote bag made from 1-inch squares, it's both practical and great-looking. Fall colors are used here, but you can imagine it made with pastels or a combination of two contrasting colors like red and white or blue and white. The strap, back, and lining are made from one of the calico prints, and the finished bag is a nice roomy 13½ inches square. This is great as a baby bag for carrying all your travel necessities. It also makes a nice shower gift filled with diapers, powder, lotion, and such. It is also the perfect size for a book bag.

MATERIALS

scraps of printed fabric
⅔ yard brown calico for back, straps, and lining
thin quilt batting
tracing paper
cardboard or acetate

DIRECTIONS

All fabric measurements for cutting include ¼-inch seam allowance.

1. Trace the pattern (Figure 1) and transfer to cardboard to make a template. Seam allowance is included.
2. Cut the following:

   From a variety of dark prints and solids:
   221 squares, each 1½ inches

   From calico:
   2 pieces, each 3½ × 33½ inches for straps
   1 piece, 14 × 14 inches, for back
   2 pieces, 14 × 14 inches, for lining

TO MAKE ROWS

1. With right sides facing and raw edges aligned, stitch 2 squares together along one side edge. Press seams to one side.
2. Refer to Figure 2. Repeat with another square to make Row 1.
3. Follow the figure to make 19 rows of squares. Open all seams and press.
4. With right sides facing and raw edges aligned, join a square to the top of the center square in Row 1 and another square to the center square of Row 19 as shown. Press all seams to one side.

TO JOIN ROWS

1. With right sides facing and raw edges aligned, pin Row 1 to Row 2 and stitch along bottom edge to join as shown.
2. Continue joining all 19 rows in this way. Press seams to one side.

TO MAKE BAG

1. From the patchwork fabric that you have just completed, cut a 14 × 14-inch square on the diagonal as shown by the dotted lines in Figure 2.
2. With right sides facing and raw edges aligned, stitch the front and back of the tote bag together around the sides and bottom, leaving the top edge open.
3. Trim seams and clip corners. Turn right side out.

TO MAKE LINING

1. Cut 2 pieces of quilt batting slightly smaller all around than the lining pieces.
2. Place a piece of batting on the wrong side of the front and back lining pieces, and with right sides of fabric facing, pin all 4 layers together.
3. Stitch around sides and bottom edges, just barely catching the batting in the seam line.

4. Trim seams and clip corners. Do not turn.
5. Slip the lining inside the patchwork tote and adjust so the side and bottom seams are aligned.

TO MAKE STRAP

1. With right sides facing and raw edges aligned, fold the long fabric strips in half lengthwise. Press.
2. Stitch along one long edge, using ¼-inch seam allowance.
3. Turn right side out and press.

Tip:

To easily turn a long strip inside out, attach a safety pin to one edge and weave the head of the pin through the fabric to the other end. Ease the fabric over itself as you pull the safety pin through the channel.

---

4. Stitch along the outside edges on the right side of the fabric.
5. Repeat Steps 1 to 4 for the second strip.

TO FINISH

1. Turn raw edges around the top of the tote and lining ¼-inch to the inside and press.
2. Fold each strap in half lengthwise. Measure 3 inches in from the side seams of the bag and pin each end of one strap between the outside and lining of the front of the tote.
3. Repeat on the back.
4. Machine-stitch around the top edge of the bag. Refer to the color photo for the finished tote.

Figure 1. Pattern.

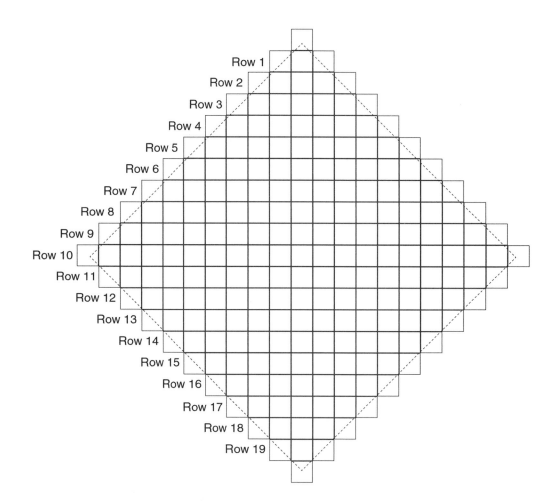

Row 1
Row 2
Row 3
Row 4
Row 5
Row 6
Row 7
Row 8
Row 9
Row 10
Row 11
Row 12
Row 13
Row 14
Row 15
Row 16
Row 17
Row 18
Row 19

Figure 2. Make rows.

15: WOOL COVERLET

When the first American settlers made quilts, they cut up used clothing to piece together. This is still the way the Amish make quilts, and now and then a quilter will cut up her children's used clothing to make a "memory" quilt. Most of these quilts were and are made of cotton or polyester material. However, men's wool slacks, jackets, and flannel shirts were used as well, and I thought it might be a fun to try a modern interpretation. Old blankets, jackets, pants, and flannel shirts can provide material, or if you don't have used clothing on hand, consider buying ¼- or ½-yard pieces of a variety of different wool and flannel fabrics. Used clothing from a thrift shop can provide an inexpensive source of material for recycling in this way. The backing can be made from a solid piece of one of the fabrics, or you can use a thin, fleece blanket for the back. The finished size is 49 × 64 inches.

Another idea for this project is a child's blanket made from a patchwork of other, worn "blankies" that your child has outgrown. It's a wonderful way to preserve the warm feelings these baby blankets once provided. If a group of quilters is making a shower gift, consider having each person contribute their own pieces to create a very personal project.

MATERIALS

remnants of different patterned wool and flannel fabric
backing fabric to match one of the remnants
thin quilt batting
6 yards of 2-inch-wide satin blanket binding in a color to match one of the fabrics
tracing paper
cardboard or acetate

DIRECTIONS

All fabric measurements for cutting include a ½-inch seam allowance.

1. Trace the pattern (Figure 1) and transfer to cardboard to make template. Seam allowance is included.

Figure 1. Pattern.

2. Cut a total of 108 squares, each 6 × 6 inches, using the pattern.
3. Refer to Figure 2. Begin by arranging the squares so that you have 12 rows with 9 squares in each row.
4. Rearrange the squares until you have a pleasing layout. It is usually best to alternate light and dark colors in each row.

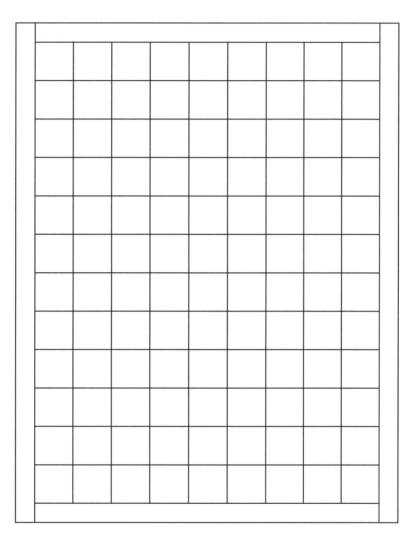

Finished Wool Coverlet.

Figure 2. Layout.

Wool Coverlet

TO MAKE ROWS

1. With right sides facing and raw edges aligned, stitch 2 squares together along one side edge. Open seams and press from the wrong side with a steam iron set at WOOL or MEDIUM HEAT.
2. Continue to add each square in this way until you have 12 rows of 9 squares each.

TO JOIN ROWS

1. With right sides facing and raw edges aligned, join Row 1 to Row 2 along the long edge, taking care to keep the seams aligned as closely as possible. Open seams and press.
2. Continue to join all rows in this way.

TO QUILT

1. Cut the batting to measure 49 × 64 inches.
2. Cut the backing fabric the same size. (See page 14 for piecing backing material, if needed.)
3. Place the batting on top of the backing fabric, then center the patchwork top over these 2 layers. There will be an additional 2 inches of batting and backing fabric around the edges. Pin all 3 layers together.
4. Baste the quilt top, batting, and backing together with long stitches through all 3 layers.
5. Since the fabric is quite thick, it's best to quilt on the sewing machine. Set the stitch length for a loose stitch, such as 6 or 8 stitches to the inch and stitch in the channel of each seam line. You might also consider simply holding the layers of fabric together with ties at various intervals.

TO FINISH

1. Trim the extra batting and backing fabric ½ inch all around.
2. Place the blanket binding over the extended batting and backing fabric so the extended fabric is encased between the binding on the front and back. Pin the

binding to the coverlet ½ inch from the raw edge all around the top pieced fabric and ½ inch from the raw edges on the back.

3. Machine- or hand-stitch all around.

16: PINE TREE WALL HANGING

Rows of staggered pine trees on a white quilted background create a handsome wall hanging. Each tree is created from the same template, using scraps of different-colored calicos. For a bold green and white design, you could use only green prints for all the trees. The finished size is 24 × 26 inches and makes a stunning Christmas decoration over a fireplace.

Quilting Club Tip:

Get together to make this project as a raffle prize for a Christmas bazaar. Each person can make one of the 13 tree blocks.

MATERIALS

All fabric is 45 inches wide.
1 yard white solid
1 yard green calico for backing
⅛ yard dark green calico for tree trunks
scraps of calicos for treetops
thin quilt batting 24 × 26 inches
tracing paper
cardboard or acetate
light pencil or fabric marker
Velcro tabs for hanging

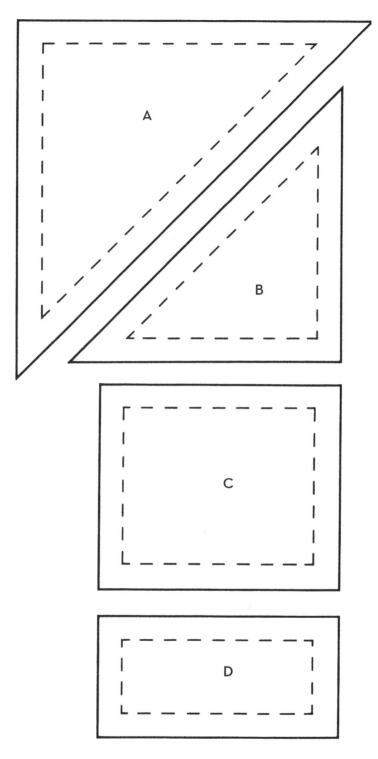

Figure 1. Patterns A to F.

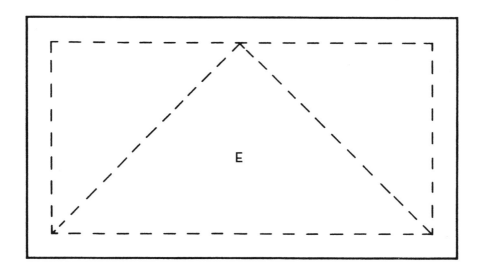

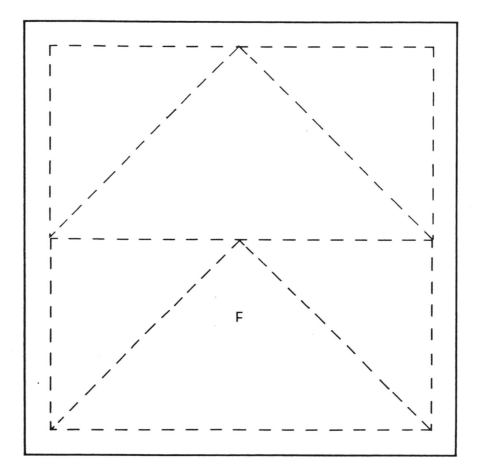

DIRECTIONS

All measurements include a ¼-inch seam allowance.

1. Trace Patterns A–F (Figure 1) and transfer to cardboard to make templates.
2. Cut the following:

   From white solid:
   2 strips, each 2 × 25½ inches (side borders)
   2 strips, each 2 × 20½ inches (top and bottom borders)
   52 triangles using Pattern B
   26 squares using Pattern C
   8 squares using Pattern E
   4 squares using Pattern F

   From green calico backing fabric:
   backing piece, 25 × 27 inches

   From dark green calico:
   13 rectangles using Pattern D

   From calico scraps:
   26 triangles using Pattern A (2 each of 13 different fabrics)

TO MAKE A BLOCK

1. Refer to Figure 2. With right sides facing, stitch the long edge of one white B piece to one short edge of an A piece. Press seams to one side.
2. Stitch another B piece to the other short edge of the A piece to make a rectangle, as shown. Press seams to one side.
3. Using the same color A piece, repeat Step 1.
4. Refer to Figure 3. With right sides facing, stitch the right side edge of a white C piece to the left long edge of a dark green calico D piece. Then, stitch the right side of the D piece to the left side of another white C piece. Press seams to one side.
5. Refer to Figure 4. With right sides facing, stitch all 3 sections together to make a tree block as shown.
6. Press seams to one side. Make 13 tree blocks in this way.

Pine Tree Wall Hanging

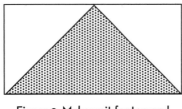

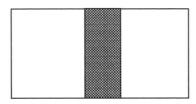

Figure 2. Make unit for top and middle of tree block.

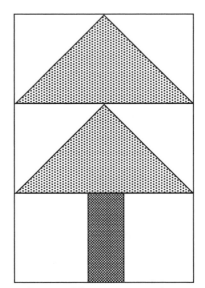

Figure 3. Make unit for bottom of tree block.

Figure 4. Three units joined to make tree block.

Figures 2 to 4. Make a block.

TO JOIN BLOCKS

Refer to Figure 5. Blocks are joined in vertical rows.

1. With right sides facing, stitch the bottom edge of a tree block to the top edge of a white E piece. Stitch the bottom edge of the white E piece to the top edge of another tree block.
2. Continue with another white E piece and then another tree block in the same way to complete vertical Row 1. Press seams to one side. Make 3 rows in this way; they will be Rows 1, 3, and 5.
3. With right sides facing, stitch the bottom edge of a white F piece to the top edge of a tree block.
4. Stitch the bottom edge of the tree block to the top edge of a white E piece.
5. Continue with another tree block and then another white F piece to complete vertical Row 2. Press seams to one side. Make 2 rows in this way; they will be Rows 2 and 4.

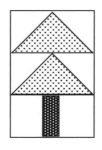

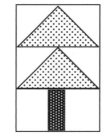

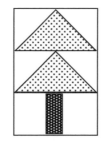

Figure 5. Make a row.

TO JOIN ROWS

1. Refer to Figure 6. With right sides facing and seams aligned, stitch the right side edge of Row 1 to the left side edge of vertical Row 2. Press seams to one side.
2. Continue with Row 3. Join all 5 rows in this way to make the quilt top. Press seams to one side.

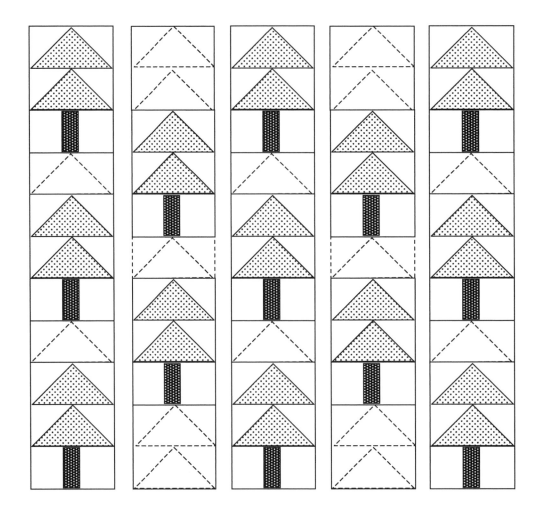

Figure 6. Join rows.

TO ADD BORDERS

1. With right sides facing, join one 2 × 2½-inch white border strip to the top edge of the quilt.
2. Join the other 2 × 20½-inch white border strip to the bottom edge of the quilt top. Press all seams.
3. With right sides facing, stitch the two 2 × 25½-inch white border strips to the sides of the quilt top in the same way. Press seams.

TO QUILT

1. Refer to Figure 7. Position the A template on the fabric as shown. Using a ruler and a light pencil or a fabric marker, mark around the template to draw the tree shapes on the white background (E and F units) between the calico trees.
2. Cut the backing piece 1-inch larger than the quilt top all around.
3. With wrong sides facing, pin the quilt top, batting, and backing together.
4. Baste through all 3 layers with long, loose stitches in a starburst pattern.
5. Using small running stitches, quilt along the premarked lines and ⅛ inch on the outside of all seam lines of each calico tree.

TO FINISH

1. When all quilting has been completed, remove basting stitches.
2. Trim the batting ½-inch smaller than the quilt top all around.
3. Turn the raw edges of the backing to the inside ¼ inch on each side and press. Next, fold the backing forward over the top edge of the quilt to create a ½-inch green border all around. Slip-stitch to the quilt top.
4. Attach a Velcro tab to the back of each corner and in the center of each side. Attach corresponding tabs to the wall where it will hang. See Figure 7 for the finished Pine Tree Wall Hanging.

Figure 7. Finished Pine Tree Wall Hanging.

17: FAIR AND SQUARE QUILT

The name for this quilt best describes its no-nonsense, straightforward design. Because the squares are fairly large and the pattern is simple, this is one of the easiest quilts in the book. It can be made with different-color solid fabrics, a combination of solid and prints, or a variety of different printed fabrics. It will look good in any color scheme.

The overall quilting gives it texture, and because the blocks are set on the diagonal and the finished size is 68 inches square, this project has a unique look. You can do as much or as little hand quilting as you like. The quilt fits either a single or full-size bed. If you want to enlarge it, simply add another border approximately 8 inches all around and you'll add 16 inches to both the length and the width.

Quilting Club Tip:

Since there are 16 identical blocks in this quilt, it is an ideal project for 4 people to work on together. Each quilter makes 4 blocks before joining them together.

MATERIALS

All fabric is 45 inches wide.
¾ yard yellow fabric A
1⅔ yards light blue fabric B
1¼ yards rose fabric C
2 yards red fabric D
4 yards backing fabric
quilt backing
tracing paper
cardboard or acetate

Figure 1. Pattern.

DIRECTIONS

All measurements include a ¼-inch seam allowance.

1. Trace the pattern (Figure 1) and transfer to cardboard to make a template. Seam allowance is included.
2. Cut the following:

   From yellow A:
       32 squares, each 5 × 5 inches

   From light blue B:
       2 pieces, each 4 × 58½ inches
       2 pieces, each 4 × 51½ inches
       32 squares, each 5 × 5 inches

   From rose C:
       9 squares, each 9½ × 9½ inches
       6 squares, each 10 × 10 inches; cut each square into 2 triangles
       1 square 10½ × 10½ inches; cut into 4 triangles

   From red D (borders):
       2 strips, each 5½ × 68½ inches
       2 strips, each 5½ × 58½ inches

TO MAKE A BLOCK

1. Refer to Figure 2. With right sides facing and raw edges aligned, stitch a yellow A square to a blue B square along the right, side edge. Open seams and press. Make 2.
2. With right sides facing and raw edges aligned, join the 2 pieces. Open seams and press. Make 16 blocks in this way.

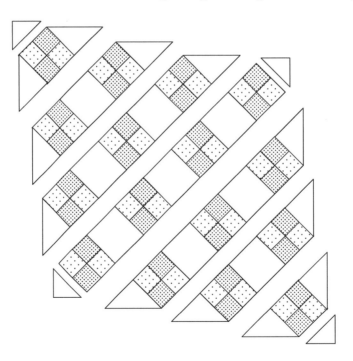

Figure 2. Make a block.

TO MAKE A ROW

1. Refer to Figure 3. With right sides facing and raw edges aligned, stitch the short end of a rose C triangle to each side of a blue-yellow block. Open seams and press.
2. To make Row 2, stitch the short side of a rose C triangle to one side of a blue-yellow block, followed by a rose C square, then another blue-yellow block, ending the row with a rose C triangle as shown. Open seams and press.
3. Continue to make all 7 rows according to Figure 3. Open seams and press.

Figure 3. Make rows.

TO JOIN ROWS

1. Refer to Figure 4. With right sides facing and raw edges aligned, stitch the long edge of a small rose C triangle to the top edge of the blue-yellow block in Row 1.
2. Stitch all 7 rows together as shown.
3. With right sides facing and raw edges aligned, join the long edge of a small rose C triangle to the bottom edge of the blue-yellow block in Row 7 and to each end of Row 4. Open seams and press.

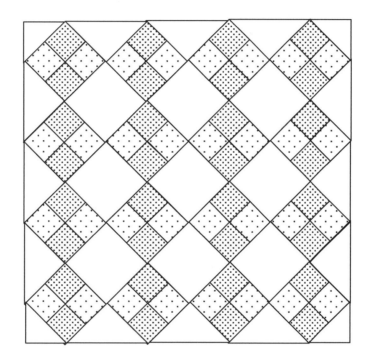

Figure 4. Join rows.

Fair and Square Quilt

TO ADD BORDERS

1. Refer to Figure 5. With right sides facing and raw edges aligned, stitch a light blue B strip (4 × 51½ inches) to the top edge of the quilt. Open seams and press. Repeat on the bottom edge.
2. Join a light blue B strip (4 × 58½ inches) to each side edge in the same way.
3. With right sides facing and raw edges aligned, join a red D strip (5½ × 58½ inches) to the top edge of the quilt. Open seams and press. Repeat on the bottom edge.
4. With right sides facing and raw edges aligned, stitch a red D strip (5½ × 68½ inches) to the sides in the same way. Open seams and press.

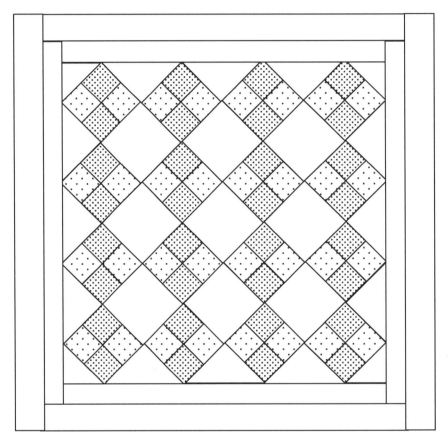

Finished Fair and Square Quilt.

Figure 5. Add borders.

TO QUILT

1. Cut the backing fabric in half so you have 2 pieces 2 yards each.
2. Stitch these 2 pieces together along the long edge.
3. You can either quilt over the entire fabric or take small running stitches on each side of all seam lines. To quilt the entire fabric with a grid pattern, see page 17.
4. With wrong sides facing and batting between, pin backing and quilt top together.
5. Starting at the center and moving outward in a sunburst pattern, baste together with long stitches.
6. Begin at the center of the quilt and take small running stitches along all premarked quilting lines.

TO FINISH

1. Remove all basting stitches.
2. Remove markings with a plant mister or dab with a damp sponge.
3. Trim the batting ¼ inch smaller than the quilt top all around.
4. Trim the backing to the same size as the quilt top.
5. Turn the raw edges of the top and backing ¼ inch to the inside and press. Pin all around and machine- or slip-stitch to finish.

18: SOFT AS A CLOUD BABY QUILT

A wonderful gift for a newborn is a soft, cuddly quilt that isn't too large to wrap the precious bundle to take home from the hospital. This quilt is just the right size to fit in the carriage or car seat. It's easy to make in a weekend, as the finished size is 24 × 32 inches, and it is quilted with tied knots in the center of the blocks rather than hand quilting. Use cotton solids and prints or choose soft flannel fabric. The ruffled edge is an optional detail.

Quilting Club Tip:

To make this project as a group effort to give as one gift from all, divide up the blocks for piecing and then each person can quilt one block before joining all blocks to make the quilt top. Note: One block can be made as a pillow if desired.

MATERIALS

All fabric is 45 inches wide.
¼ yard white solid fabric
¼ yard pink solid fabric
1 yard blue calico (includes backing)
1 yard batting
3¼ yards 2-inch-wide eyelet
3¼ yards 1-inch-wide eyelet
1 skein pink embroidery floss for tying
tracing paper
cardboard or acetate

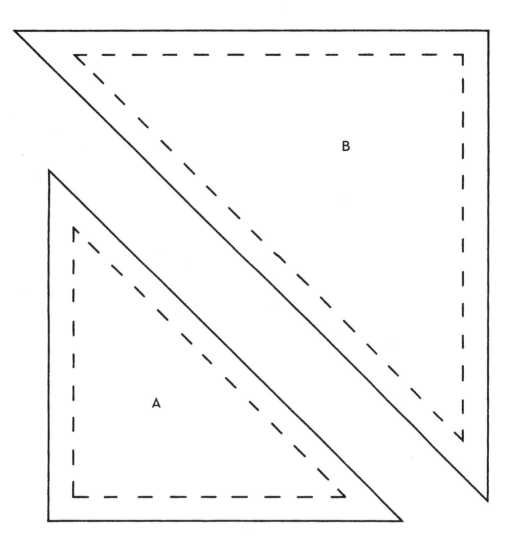

Figure 1. Patterns A and B.

DIRECTIONS

All measurements include a ¼-inch seam allowance.

1. Trace Patterns A and B (Figure 1) and transfer to cardboard to make templates. Seam allowance is included.
2. Cut the following:

From white solid:
    48 triangles from Pattern A

From pink solid:
    48 triangles from Pattern A

From blue calico:
    backing piece, 24½ × 32½ inches
    48 triangles from Pattern B

TO MAKE BLOCKS

1. Refer to Figure 2. With right sides facing, join a white A piece to a pink A piece along one short edge to make a larger triangle.
2. Open seams and press. Make 48 pieced triangles in this way.
3. Refer to Figure 3. With right sides facing, stitch a pieced triangle to a blue calico B piece along the diagonal to make a square.
4. Open seams and press. Make 48 squares in this way.

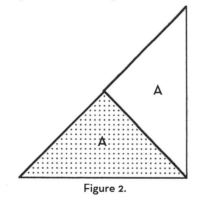

Figure 2.

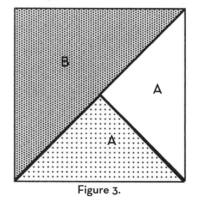

Figure 3.

Figures 2 and 3. Make a square.

5. Refer to Figure 4. With right sides facing, stitch 4 of these squares together to make a block as shown.
6. Open seams and press. Make 12 blocks in this way.

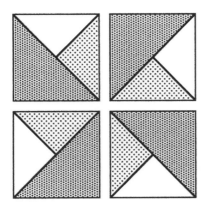 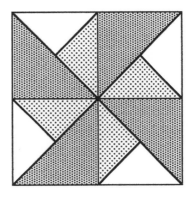

Figure 4. Make a block.

TO MAKE A ROW

1. Refer to Figure 5. With right sides facing, stitch 2 blocks together along the side edges.
2. Continue with another block to make a row of 3 blocks as shown.
3. Open seams and press. Make 4 rows in this way.

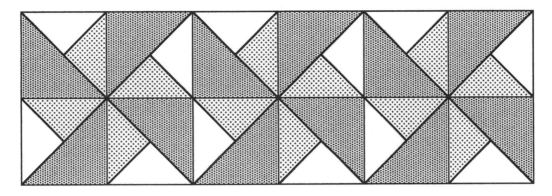

Figure 5. Make a row.

Soft as a Cloud Baby Quilt

TO JOIN ROWS

1. Refer to Figure 6. With right sides facing, stitch the bottom edge of a row to the top edge of another row.
2. Open seams and press.
3. Continue to join all 4 rows in this way to make the quilt top.

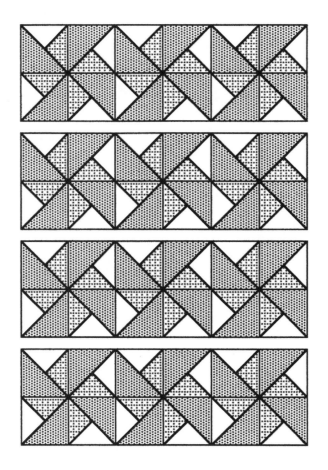

Figure 6. Join rows.

TO ADD EYELET TRIM

1. With raw edges matching, pin the 1-inch-wide eyelet to the front of the 2-inch-wide eyelet and stitch across the raw edge to join.
2. With right sides facing and raw edges aligned, pin the raw edge of the eyelet to the quilt top all around. Overlap the ends where they meet.
3. Stitch all around.

TO FINISH

1. With right sides facing, pin the backing and the quilt top together with the eyelet between.
2. Center this over the quilt batting and pin all 3 layers together. There will be extra batting all around.
3. Trim the excess batting to the same size as the fabric.
4. Stitch around 4 corners and 3 sides, leaving the bottom edge open for turning. Turn right side out.
5. Turn the raw edges of the opening to the inside ¼ inch and press.
6. Slip-stitch the open edge closed, or machine-stitch across.
7. Use the embroidery floss to tie the center of each block in the following way: Cut a length of floss 12 inches and thread it through the needle, leaving a 5-inch tail. Do not make a knot on the end. Insert the needle through the top of the quilt in the center of the first block, then up again in the same spot. Make a knot, then a bow, and cut the ends of the floss. You will need approximately 6 inches for each bow.
8. Repeat in the center of each block. If you want to add hand quilting, take small running stitches along each side of each seam through all 3 layers of fabric. See Figure 7 for the finished Soft as a Cloud Quilt.

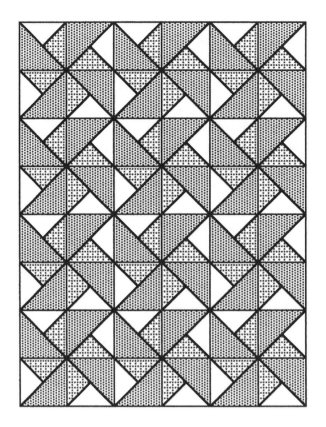

Figure 7. Finished Soft as a Cloud Quilt.

19: PINK SAILS QUILT

This is a familiar pattern, usually made with shades of blue for a boy's room. The use of pink and white is a twist that makes this a delightfully feminine quilt as well as a pretty wall hanging. This is a full-size bed quilt with finished measurements of 76 × 88 inches. Make it with fewer blocks and it can become a crib quilt, or use the pattern for one block to make a pillow. While this is a large project, the quick and easy triangle method is used for a shortcut to piecing triangles into squares.

> **Quilting Club Tip:**
>
> This is a good project for a group to work on together. Each person can make one block of the sailboat or you might break down the steps so that one person is doing all the measuring and another the cutting while another pins the pieces together for someone else to do all the machine stitching. Each person hands her work off to the next person for subsequent steps.

MATERIALS

All fabric is 45 inches wide.
2 yards white fabric A
4½ yards pink fabric B
5 yards backing fabric
quilt batting 76 × 88 inches

DIRECTIONS

All measurements include a ¼-inch seam allowance.

Cut the following:

From white A:
> 4 strips, each 3½ × 60½ inches
> 1 piece, 25 × 30 inches
> 13 rectangles, each 3½ × 12½ inches
> 26 rectangles, each 3½ × 6½ inches

From pink B:
> 2 strips, each 3½ × 60½ inches
> 2 strips, each 8½ × 76½ inches
> 2 strips, each 3½ × 88½ inches
> 1 rectangle, 25 × 30 inches
> 13 rectangles, each 3½ × 6½ inches
> 12 squares, each 12½ × 12½ inches

QUICK AND EASY TRIANGLE METHOD

1. On the wrong side of the white fabric, measure and mark a grid of squares, each 3⅞ × 3⅞ inches, to create 6 rows of 7 squares each.
2. With right sides facing, pin the marked fabric to the same-size pink fabric and refer to page 19 for stitching and cutting directions.
3. You will have 84 pink and white squares although you'll need only 78. Some quilters feel it's good to have a few extra.

TO MAKE SAILBOAT BLOCK

For top section of block:
1. Refer to Figure 1. With right sides facing and raw edges aligned, stitch along one side edge to join 2 pink and white squares to make Row 1. Press seams to one side.
2. Repeat with 2 more squares to make Row 2.
3. With right sides facing and raw edges aligned, stitch across bottom edge to join the two rows.
4. With right sides facing, join a 3½ × 6½-inch pink B rectangle to the left side edge of the pieced squares. Press seams to one side.
5. Repeat on the opposite side edge in the same way to complete the top half of the sailboat block.

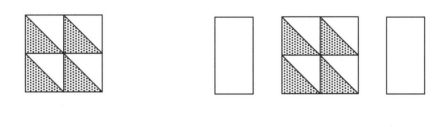

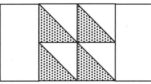

Figure 1. Make top section of block.

For bottom section of block:
6. Refer to Figure 2. With right sides facing, join a pink and white square to a 3½ × 6½-inch pink B rectangle along one short end, followed by another pink and white square as shown on the other short end. Press seams to one side.
7. With right sides facing and raw edges aligned, join this strip to a white A 3½ × 12½-inch rectangle along a long edge as shown. Press seams to one side to complete the bottom half of the block.

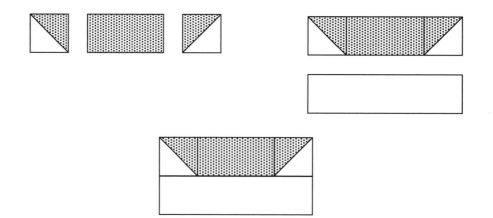

Figure 2. Make bottom section of block.

8. Refer to Figures 3 and 4. With right sides facing and seams aligned, join the top and bottom halves of the block to make the sailboat. Press seams to one side. Make 13 blocks in this way.

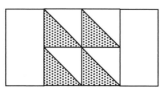

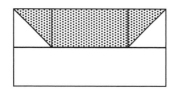

Figure 3. Join top and bottom sections of block.   **Figure 4. Finished block.**

Crayon Triangles for Baby (page 97)

Patchwork Tote (page 103)

Wool Coverlet (page 107)

Pine Tree Wall Hanging (page 112)

Fair and Square Quilt (page 121)

Soft as a Cloud Baby Quilt (page 128)

Floral Sachets (page 143)

Pink Sails Quilt (page 135)

Christmas Throw (page 149)

Homespun Star Quilt and Pillows (pages 157 and 167)

Holiday Quilt (page 170)

Holiday Pillow (page 179)

TO MAKE ROWS

1. Refer to Figure 5. With right sides facing and raw edges aligned, join a sailboat block to a pink B square 12½ × 12½ inches along the right side edge. Press seams to one side.
2. With right sides facing, pin and stitch a sailboat block to the right side of the square, followed by a pink B square and ending the row with another sailboat block. Press all seams to one side. Make 3 rows in this way for Rows 1, 3, and 5.
3. To make Row 2, begin with a pink B square, then a sailboat block, followed by a pink B square, another sailboat block, and ending with a pink B square. Press seams to one side. Make 2 rows in this way for Rows 2 and 4.

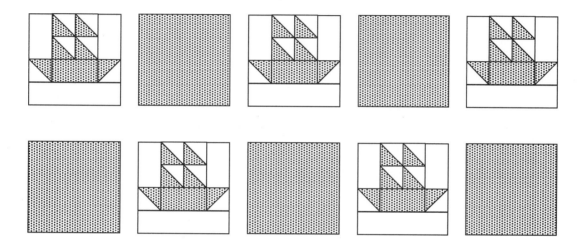

Figure 5. Make rows.

TO JOIN ROWS

1. Refer to Figure 6. With right sides facing and seams aligned, join Row 1 with Row 2 along one long edge. Press seams to one side.
2. Continue to join rows in this way.

Figure 6. Assembly.

TO JOIN BORDERS

1. With right sides facing, pin a white A strip (3½ × 60½ inches) to the bottom edge of the quilt top and stitch across. Press seams to one side.
2. Repeat on the top edge of the quilt in the same way.
3. With right sides facing, join a pink B strip (3½ × 60½ inches) to the bottom edge of the quilt top. Press seams to one side.
4. Repeat on the top edge of the quilt in the same way.
5. Repeat Steps 1 and 2.
6. With right sides facing, join a pink B strip (8½ × 76½ inches) to the bottom edge of the quilt top. Press seam to one side.
7. Repeat on the top edge of the quilt in the same way.
8. With right sides facing, join a pink B strip (8½ × 88½ inches) to one side edge of the quilt top. Press seam to one side.
9. Repeat on the opposite side edge to complete the quilt top.

TO QUILT

1. For a simple quilting pattern, consider creating a diagonal grid of evenly spaced lines across the quilt borders. (See page 17.)
2. With wrong sides facing and batting between, pin the backing, batting, and quilt top together. There will be extra backing fabric all around.
3. Beginning at the center and working outward in a sunburst pattern, take long, loose basting stitches through all 3 layers, stopping short of the seam allowance around the outer edges.
4. Using small running stitches, quilt along all premarked quilting lines or ¼ inch on each side of all seam lines. Do not quilt into the seam allowance around the quilt.

TO FINISH

1. When all quilting is complete, remove basting stitches.
2. Trim the batting ¼ inch smaller than the quilt top all around.
3. Trim the backing to same size as quilt top.
4. Turn backing edges to inside ¼ inch and press.

Pink Sails Quilt

5. Turn raw edges of quilt top to inside ¼ inch and press.
6. Slip-stitch or machine-stitch all around to finish. See Figure 7 for the finished Pink Sails Quilt.

Figure 7. Finished Pink Sails Quilt.

20: FLORAL SACHETS

Pretty patchwork sachets are fun to make and give as gifts or use to scent your dresser drawers, closets, and linens. I used pastel floral prints combined with striped fabric and solid pastels and edged each pillow sachet with eyelet ruffles. Each finished project is 6 inches square without the 2- or 3-inch ruffle. There are 3 different designs that are quick and easy to make from scraps of fabric. All the designs are made from squares or triangles pieced into squares. Ask a few of your friends over for a "Patchwork Party" and make a batch to sell at your next PTA or fund-raising event. They'll disappear faster than a plate of brownies.

MATERIALS

small amounts each of a floral print, a striped fabric, and a pastel in colors
    that go together
1 yard 2- or 3-inch-wide pregathered, eyelet ruffle for each sachet
1 yard piping if desired
6½ × 6½-inch backing fabric for each sachet
premixed potpourri or Poly-Fil stuffing for each pillow
tracing paper
cardboard or acetate

DIRECTIONS

All measurements include a ¼-inch seam allowance.
Trace Patterns A and B (Figure 1) and transfer to cardboard to make templates.

Sachet 1

Cut the following:

From the floral print:
    4 triangles using Pattern A
    1 square using Pattern B

From the striped fabric:
    4 squares using Pattern B

From the solid pastel:
    4 triangles using Pattern A

Sachet 2

Cut the following:

From the floral print:
    4 triangles using Pattern A
    4 squares using Pattern B

From the striped fabric:
    4 triangles using Pattern A
    1 square using Pattern B

Sachet 3

Cut the following:

From the floral fabric:
    9 triangles using Pattern A

From the striped fabric:
    9 triangles using Pattern A

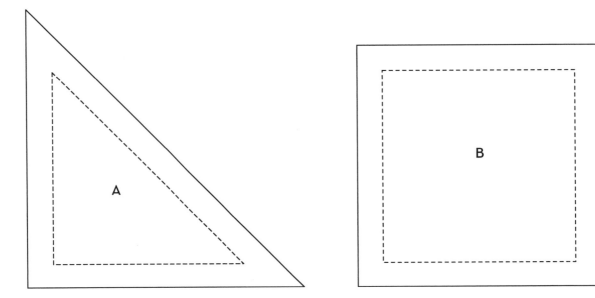

Figure 1. Patterns.

TO ASSEMBLE SACHET 1

Note: This is a pinwheel design. Refer to Figure 2 for placement of squares.

1. With right sides facing, join a floral A piece to a solid pastel A piece along the diagonal to make a square.
2. Press seams to one side. Make 4 squares in this way.
3. With right sides facing, join a pieced square to a striped B square along one side edge. Press seams to one side.
4. To complete Row 1, join another striped B square to the opposite side of the pieced square.
5. To make Row 2, join a pieced square to each side edge of a floral B square in the same way.
6. To make Row 3, join a striped B square to each side edge of a pieced square.
7. With right sides facing and seams aligned, join all 3 rows to complete the sachet top as shown. Refer to Figure 3.

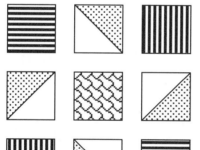

Figure 2. Sachet 1: Make squares.

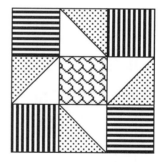

Figure 3. Sachet 1: Join rows to finish sachet.

Figures 2 and 3.

Floral Sachets

TO ASSEMBLE SACHET 2

Refer to Figure 4.

1. With right sides facing, join a floral A piece to a striped A piece along the diagonal to make a square.
2. Press seams to one side. Make 4 squares in this way.
3. With right sides facing, join a pieced square to a floral B square along one side edge. Press seams to one side.
4. Join another pieced square to the opposite side of the floral B square to complete Row 1 as shown. Press seams to one side.
5. To make Row 2, join a floral B square to each side edge of a striped B square as shown. Press seams to one side.
6. To make Row 3, join a pieced square to each side edge of a floral B square as shown. Press seams to one side.
7. With right sides facing and seams aligned, join Row 1 and Row 2 along one edge. Open seams and press. Join Row 3 to Row 2 to complete the patchwork top as shown in Figure 5. Press seams.

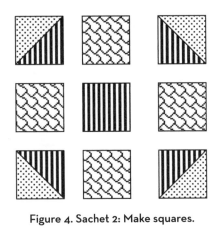

Figure 4. Sachet 2: Make squares.

Figure 5. Sachet 2:
Join rows to finish sachet.

Figures 4 and 5.

TO ASSEMBLE SACHET 3

Note: When piecing stripes and floral triangles, be sure the stripes are all positioned in the same direction. Refer to Figure 6.

1. With right sides facing, join a striped A piece to a floral A piece along the diagonal to make a square. Press seams to one side. Make 9 squares in this way.
2. Arrange the squares in 3 rows of 3 squares each with the floral triangles on the left and stripes on the right.
3. With right sides facing, join the squares to make rows.
4. With right sides facing and seams aligned, join all 3 rows as shown in Figure 7.

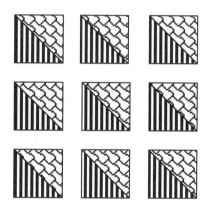

Figure 6. Sachet 3: Make squares.

Figure 7. Sachet 3: Join rows to finish sachet.

Figures 6 and 7.

TO FINISH ALL SACHETS

1. With right sides facing and raw edges aligned, stitch the piping around the patch-work top of each sachet.
2. With right sides facing and raw edges aligned, pin the eyelet ruffle around the sachet top.
3. Using the piping stitches as a guide, join the eyelet ruffle to the sachet top.
4. With right sides facing and ruffle between, pin the backing fabric to the sachet top.
5. Stitch around 3 sides and 4 corners, leaving 3 inches open for turning and stuffing.
6. Clip corners and trim seam allowance. Turn right side out and press if needed.
7. Fill each sachet with your favorite potpourri mixture or fiber-fill stuffing to which you have added a drop or two of perfume.
8. Turn the raw edges of the opening to the inside and slip-stitch closed.

21: CHRISTMAS THROW

It's fun to make a small quilted throw for the holidays using bright Christmas colors. This patchwork can be used on a table, on the wall, or over a sofa to cheer your home. We made ours with red, white, and green prints. If you use colors to match your room, the throw will have an entirely different look.

This project looks difficult, but it is one of the easier ones in the book because it's made with the quick and easy triangle method. No one will guess that even during the busiest month of the year you could create dramatic holiday decoration in just a weekend. Then you'll be able to take your time hand quilting the top during the more relaxed winter months.

The finished size is 43 × 43 inches. Since most quilting fabric is 45 inches wide, you won't have to piece the backing material. The finished project requires only 4½ yards of fabric including the backing.

Quilting Club Tip:

Since this quilt is made up of 9 blocks, it is a good project to work on with 2 friends. Each person will have 3 identical blocks to complete. If there are more members of your quilting group, have one person cut out the fabric pieces, another pin fabric pieces together, while another does the machine stitching.

MATERIALS

All fabric is 45 inches wide.
1 yard green print fabric
1½ yards white fabric
2 yards red print fabric (includes backing)
quilt batting 45 × 45 inches
yardstick

DIRECTIONS

All measurements include a ¼-inch seam allowance.

Quick and Easy Triangle Method
1. On the wrong side of the white fabric, measure and mark a grid of 80 squares, each 3⅞ × 3⅞ inches, with 8 rows of 10 squares each.
2. With right sides facing, pin this fabric to the same-size green fabric. Refer to page 19 for stitching and cutting directions.
3. On the wrong side of the white fabric, measure and mark a grid of 18 squares, each 3⅞ × 3⅞ inches, so you have 6 rows of 3 squares each.
4. With right sides facing, pin this fabric to the same-size red fabric. Refer to page 19 for stitching and cutting directions.

TO MAKE A BLOCK

1. Refer to Figure 1 to arrange rows of green-white squares and red-white squares.
2. With right sides facing, join 4 green-white squares to make Row 1 as shown. Press seams to one side.
3. Next, join a white-green square to a red-white square along the right side edge as shown, followed by another red-white square and ending Row 2 with a green-white square. Press seams to one side.
4. With right sides facing, join a white-green square to a red-white square, followed by another red-white square and ending Row 3 with a green-white square. Press seams to one side.
5. With right sides facing, join 4 green-white squares as shown to make Row 4. Press seams to one side.
6. Refer to Figure 2. With right sides facing and seams aligned, join the rows to make a block as shown. Make 9 blocks in this way.

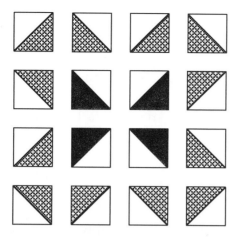

Figure 1. Arrange squares in rows then join rows to make block.

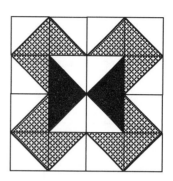

Figure 2.

Figures 1 and 2. Make a block.

TO PIECE BORDERS

1. Refer to Figure 3. With right sides facing, join a green-white square to another green/white square along one edge as shown. Press seam to one side.
2. Continue to join 12 squares in this way. Make 2 for side borders.
3. To make top and bottom borders: With right sides facing, join a green-white square to another green-white square along one edge as shown. Press seam to one side.
4. Continue to join 14 squares in this way. Make 2 borders.

Top and bottom border

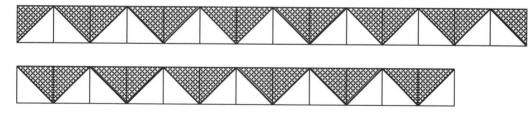

Side borders

Figure 3. Join border pieces.

Christmas Throw

TO JOIN BLOCKS

1. Refer to Figure 4. With right sides facing, join 2 blocks along the right side edge. Press seam to one side.
2. Next, join another block in the same way to make a row of 3 blocks as shown.
3. Press seam to one side. Make 3 rows in this way.

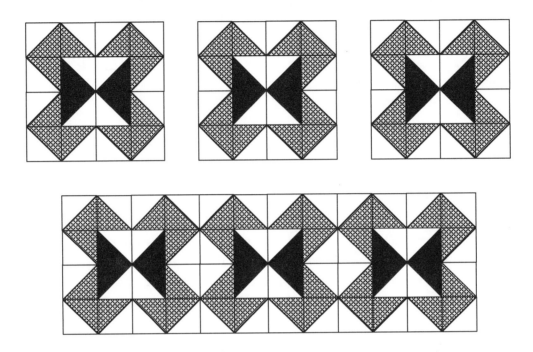

Figure 4. Make a row.

TO JOIN ROWS

1. Refer to Figure 5. With right sides facing and seams aligned, join the bottom edge of the first row to the top edge of the second row.
2. Press seams to one side.
3. Join the last row in the same way.

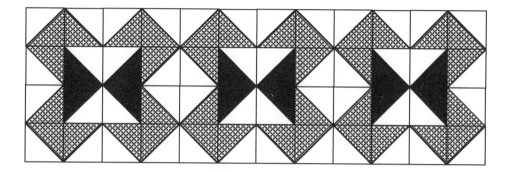

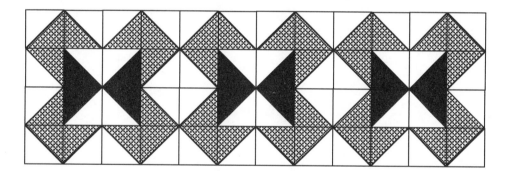

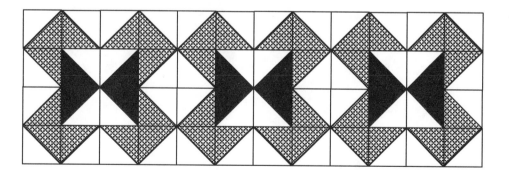

Figure 5. Join rows.

Christmas Throw

TO JOIN BORDERS

1. Refer to Figure 6. With right sides facing, join a side border strip to the left side edge of the quilt top as shown.
2. Press seam to one side.
3. Repeat on the opposite side edge.
4. With right sides facing, join a top border strip to the top edge of the quilt as shown.
5. Press seam to one side.
6. Repeat on the bottom edge of the quilt top with the remaining border strip.

Figure 6. Join borders.

TO QUILT

1. With wrong sides facing and batting between, pin the backing, batting, and quilt top together.
2. Beginning at the center of the quilt and working outward in a sunburst pattern, take long, loose basting stitches through all 3 layers, stopping short of the seam allowance around the outside edges.
3. Take small running stitches ¼ inch from each side of all seam lines, stopping short of the seam allowance around the quilt top.

TO FINISH

1. When all quilting is complete, remove basting stitches.
2. Trim the batting ¼ inch smaller than quilt top all around.
3. Next, turn the raw edges of the backing forward ¼ inch and press.
4. Bring the remaining backing fabric forward to bind the edges of the quilt top and press. Pin all around and slip-stitch or machine-stitch to finish the quilt. See Figure 7 for the finished Christmas Throw.

Figure 7. Finished Christmas Throw.

22: HOMESPUN STAR QUILT

A star pattern seems just right for a special holiday bedcover, and this one is particularly good-looking because we used homespun fabric in red and green checks. It is one of my favorites. However, you can make this pattern with colors other than green and red to fit your bedroom color scheme and it will look every bit as nice. Even though the fabric is traditional, by using two different colors of the same fabric surrounded by white, the pattern has a contemporary look. The background of this quilt is dominated by white squares, making it light and airy. This quilt was made to fit a double or queen-size bed and is 76 × 97 inches. See the following project for matching pillows.

Quilting Club Tip:

There are many ways to divide this quilt into a terriffic group project. One person cuts all fabric pieces, or 3 people cut one color each. One person can pin all pieces together while another stitches the pinned pieces together as they are ready. Another way to divide the steps is to have each member of the group make one block. Or one person might make all the centers of the blocks while another person puts the larger blocks together. This is also a good pattern for pillows. Each member of a quilting club might want to use the same pattern but with individual colors and fabrics to make his or her own pillow. See the following project for matching pillows.

MATERIALS

All fabric is 45 inches wide.
1 yard red checked homespun fabric
2½ yards white fabric
3 yards green checked homespun fabric
5½ yards backing fabric

quilt batting
tracing paper
cardboard or acetate

DIRECTIONS

All measurements include a ¼-inch seam allowance.

1   Trace Patterns A–C (Figure 1) and transfer to cardboard to make templates. Seam
    allowance is included.
2. Cut the following:

From red:
    1 rectangle, 36 × 45 inches

From white:
    1 rectangle, 36 × 45 inches
    48 squares using Pattern A
    48 squares using Pattern B
    24 squares using Pattern C (cut each square into 4 triangles)

From green:
    Borders:
        2 strips, each 8½ × 60½ inches
        2 strips, each 8½ × 97½ inches
    Lattice strips:
        8 strips, each 3½ × 18½ inches
        3 strips, each 3½ × 60½ inches
    12 squares using Pattern B
    24 squares using Pattern C (cut each square into 4 triangles)

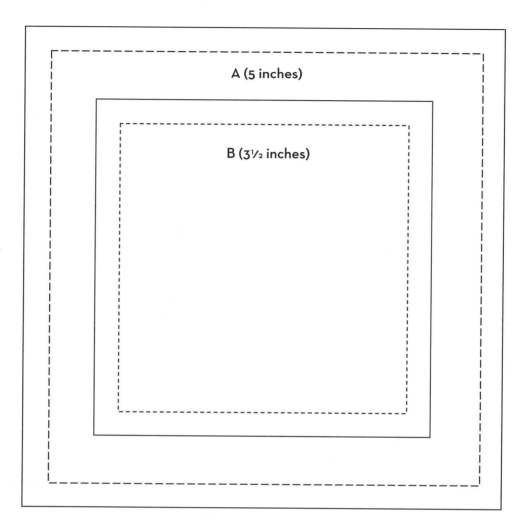

A (5 inches)

B (3½ inches)

Figure 1. Patterns A to C.

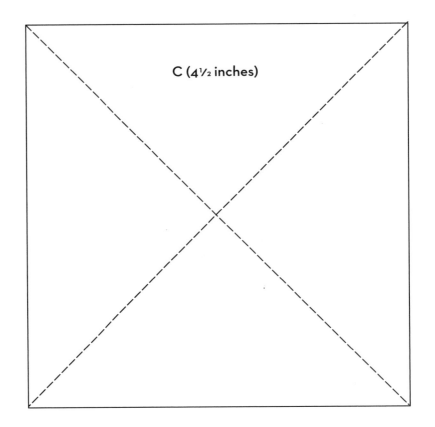

C (4½ inches)

TO MAKE A SQUARE

1. Refer to Figure 2. With right sides facing and raw edges aligned, stitch a green triangle to a white triangle along one edge to make a larger triangle. Make 96. Open seams and press.
2. Stitch 2 pieced triangles together to make a square as shown. Make 48. Open seams and press.

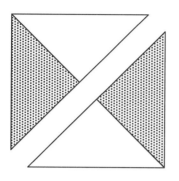

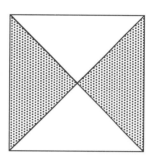

Figure 2. Make a square.

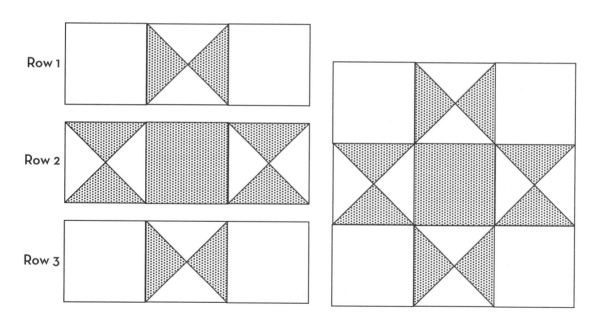

Row 1

Row 2

Row 3

Figure 3. Make the center block.

Homespun Star Quilt

TO MAKE THE GREEN CENTER BLOCK

1. Refer to Figure 3. With right sides facing and raw edges aligned, join a small white B square to a green and white square along one edge. Open seams and press.
2. Next, join another white B square to the green and white square in the same way to complete Row 1 of 3 squares. Open seams and press.
3. For Row 2, join a green and white square to a green B square and then complete the row with a green and white square as shown.
4. Repeat Row 1 to make Row 3.
5. With right sides facing and raw edges aligned, pin the bottom edge of Row 1 to the top edge of Row 2 and stitch across. Open seams and press.
6. Join Row 3 to the bottom edge of Row 2 in the same way. This is the star square and the center of the block.

QUICK AND EASY TRIANGLE METHOD

Refer to Figure B, page 19.
1. Mark 96 squares, each 5½ × 5½ inches, on the wrong side of the large white fabric (36 × 45 inches). Draw a diagonal line through all squares.
2. With right sides facing, pin this to the same-size piece of red checked fabric. Stitch ¼ inch in on each side of the diagonal lines.
3. Cut on all solid lines. Open seams and press. You should have 96 squares made of red and white triangles. Open all seams and press.

TO MAKE A BLOCK

1. Refer to Figure 4. With right sides facing and raw edges aligned, stitch 2 red and white squares together as shown for left side of block. Open seams and press.
2. Repeat on right side.
3. Repeat with 2 red and white squares for top and bottom as shown.
4. With right sides facing and raw edges aligned, join a 5½-inch white A square to each side edge of the top and bottom strips as shown. Press seams to dark side.
5. With right sides facing and raw edges aligned, join side squares to the center block in the same way. Repeat with the remaining top and bottom pieced strips as shown. Open seams and press. Make 12.

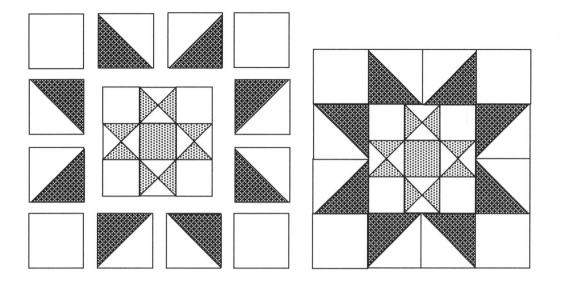

Figure 4. Make the outer star.

TO MAKE ROWS

1. Refer to Figure 5. With right sides facing and raw edges aligned, join a green lattice strip (3½ × 18½ inches) to a block along the right side edge. Open seams and press.
2. Next, join a block in the same way following by another lattice strip and another block to complete Row 1.
3. Continue to join blocks in this way until you have 4 rows of 3 blocks each.

Figure 5. Make a row.

Homespun Star Quilt

TO JOIN ROWS

1. Refer to Figure 6. With right sides facing and raw edges aligned, pin the top edge of a green lattice strip (3½ × 60½ inches) to the bottom edge of the first row of blocks and stitch across. Open seams and press.
2. With right sides facing, pin the top edge of the second row to the bottom edge of the lattice strip and stitch across. Open seams and press. Continue to join rows separated by lattice strips in this way. Open seams and press.

Figure 6. Join rows and borders.

TO JOIN BORDERS

1. Refer again to Figure 6. With right sides facing and raw edges aligned, pin the bottom edge of the top green border strip to the top edge of the quilt. Stitch across. Repeat on the bottom edge.
2. Next, join the side border pieces in the same way. Open seams and press.

TO FINISH

1. Cut the batting ½ inch smaller than the quilt top all around.
2. Cut the backing fabric in half so that you have 2 pieces, each 2¾ yards. Cut one piece in half lengthwise.
3. With right sides facing and raw edges aligned, join one narrow half to each side of the wider fabric piece. Trim the fabric to the size of the quilt top.
4. With wrong sides facing and batting between, pin the top, backing, and batting together.
5. Beginning in the center and moving outward in a sunburst pattern, baste all 3 layers of fabric together with long stitches.
6. To quilt by hand, take small running stitches ¼ inch in from seam lines on each side of all seams.
7. When all quilting is complete, clip away basting stitches.
8. Turn raw edges of the quilt top under ½ inch and press. Turn backing edges to inside ½ inch and press. Pin edges together all around.
9. Stitch all around with slip stitch or machine stitch. See Figure 7 for the finished Homespun Star Quilt.

Figure 7. Finished Homespun Star Quilt.

23: HOMESPUN STAR PILLOWS

If you like this pattern but feel that a quilt is too ambitious a project, start with a pillow made from one block. This will teach you the basics of patchwork as applied to making a star design. When finished, you will have made one block of the quilt. Making a pillow top will give you an idea of how much is involved in making the quilt in the previous chapter. Then decide whether to do just the pillow or proceed with the quilt. The finished size of each pillow is 18 × 18 inches. One is predominantly red, while the other uses green as the main color. They are trimmed with contrasting color piping all around. You can buy premade piping in a fabric store, but you may not be able to find it in the exact color to match your fabric. I've, therefore. included the directions for making the piping to match your pillow.

MATERIALS (FOR A GREEN PILLOW)

For a red pillow, reverse amounts of red and green homespun.
All fabric is 45 inches wide.
¼ yard red checked homespun fabric
⅓ yard white fabric
⅔ yard green checked homespun fabric
2 yards cording
pillow form, 18 × 18 inches
tracing paper
cardboard or acetate

DIRECTIONS

All measurements include ¼-inch seam allowance.

1. Trace Patterns A–C (Figure 1, pages 159–60) and transfer to cardboard to make templates. Seam allowance is included.
2. Cut the following:

From green:

    1 square, 18½ × 18½ inches, for the back

    2 strips, each 1½ × 38 inches, to cover the cording

    1 square using Pattern B

    2 squares using Pattern C (cut each square into 4 triangles)

From white:

    4 squares using Pattern A

    4 squares using Pattern B

    2 squares using Pattern C (cut each square into 4 triangles)

    1 strip, 6 × 23 inches

TO MAKE A SQUARE

1. With right sides facing and raw edges aligned, stitch a green triangle to a white triangle to make a larger triangle. Make 8. Open seams and press.
2. Next, stitch 2 pieced triangles together along the long edge to make a square as shown in Figure 2 on page 161. Make 4. Open seams and press.
3. Refer to Figure 3 on page 161. With right sides facing and raw edges aligned, stitch a small white B square to a green and white square along one edge. Then join with a white B square to make the first row for the star square.
4. For Row 2, join a pieced square to a green B square and complete the row with a pieced square. To make Row 3, repeat Row 1.
5. With right sides together and raw edges aligned, join Row 1 and Row 2 and then Row 3 as shown to make the star square. This is the center of the block. Open seams and press.

TO MAKE THE BLOCK

The following directions are for the quick and easy triangle method. See page 19.

1. Mark 4 squares, each 5½ × 5½ inches, on the wrong side of the 6 × 23-inch strip of white fabric. Draw a diagonal line through each square.
2. With right sides facing, pin this strip to the same-size red check fabric. Stitch ¼ inch in on each side of the diagonal lines.

3. Cut on all solid lines. Open seams and press. You should have 8 squares made of red and white triangles.
4. Refer to Figure 4 on page 163. With right sides facing and raw edges aligned, stitch squares together to make the block with the star in the center as shown. Open seams and press.

TO FINISH

1. Stitch the 2 green strips of fabric together along one short end to make a long strip to cover the cording.
2. To Make Piping: Beginning ½ inch from the end of the green fabric strip, place the cording in the center of the wrong side of the strip and fold the fabric over so that the raw edges meet. With the cording encased inside the fabric, use the zipper foot on the sewing machine to stitch as close to the cording as possible.
3. With right sides facing and raw edges aligned, pin the piping around the edge of the pillow top, overlapping the raw ends of the piping fabric. Stitch around, as close to cording as possible.
4. With right sides facing and raw edges aligned, pin the backing fabric to the top of the pillow with the piping between.
5. Using the piping stitches as a guide, stitch around 3 sides and 4 corners. Trim seam allowance and clip corners. Turn right side out and press.

For the second pillow, reverse the colors: Make the star in red and white and the surrounding squares in green and white. The piping and backing will then be made with the red checked homespun.

24: HOLIDAY QUILT

This is not a typical quilt pattern, but rather a contemporary version of a traditional star. It works beautifully for a patchwork throw and matching pillow, and makes a great holiday gift. The finished quilt is 48 × 60 inches, which is perfect for a lap throw or wall hanging. Choose deep cranberry, hunter green, and black printed fabrics for a rich colonial look. While the star pattern suggests a holiday theme, if you make this quilt using a different color combination, the quilt will have an entirely different look. There are two blocks, A and B. They both use the same pattern, in reverse colors. This quilt would be a lovely gift to cheer someone in the hospital, or to donate as the raffle prize for a worthy fund-raising event. Make this quilt with a friend by designating one of you as the "A" person and the other as the "B" person. See the following project for a matching pillow.

MATERIALS

All fabric is 45 inches wide.
¼ yard dark red calico
1½ yards bright red calico
1¾ yards dark green calico
3 yards black or navy blue calico (includes backing)
quilt batting, 48 × 60 inches
tracing paper
cardboard or acetate

DIRECTIONS

All measurements include a ¼-inch seam allowance.
1. Trace Patterns A–C (Figure 1) and transfer to cardboard to make templates. Seam allowance is included.
2. Cut the following:

From dark red calico:
    12 squares using Pattern C

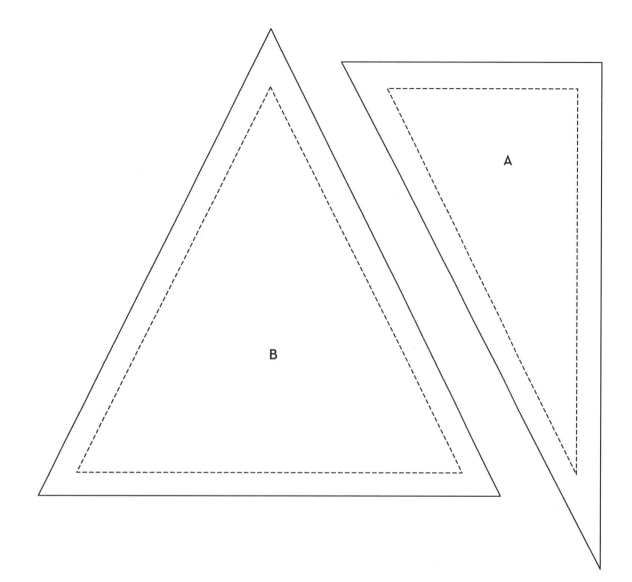

Figure 1. Patterns A to C.

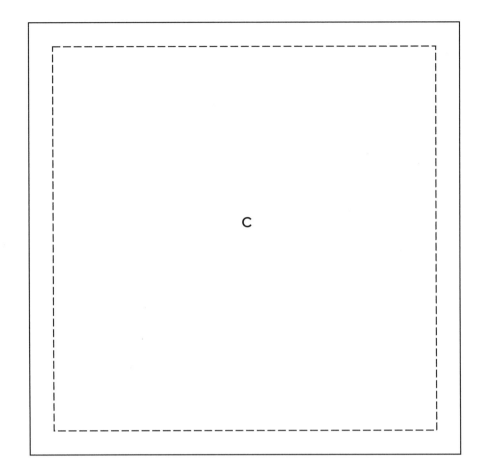

From bright red calico:
    Borders:
        2 strips, each 2½ × 36½ inches (top and bottom)
        2 strips, each 2½ × 52½ inches (sides)
    96 triangles using Pattern A

From dark green calico:
    Borders:
        2 strips, each 4½ × 40½ inches (top and bottom)
        2 strips, each 4½ × 60½ inches (sides)
    24 squares using Pattern C
    24 triangles using Pattern B

From black or navy calico:
    2 pieces, each 31 × 49 inches, for backing
    24 squares using Pattern C
    24 triangles using Pattern B

BLOCK A

1. Refer to Figure 2. With right sides facing and raw edges aligned, stitch the diagonal side of a red A triangle to each side of a black calico B triangle to make a square. This is Unit 1. Make 4.
2. Open seams and press.

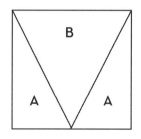

Figure 2. Make Unit 1.

TO MAKE ROWS FOR BLOCK A

1. Refer to Figure 3. With right sides facing and raw edges aligned, stitch a green calico C square to Unit 1 along one side edge. Open seams and press.
2. Stitch a green calico C square to the opposite side of Unit 1 to make Row 1 of Block A.
3. With right sides facing and raw edges aligned, stitch Unit 1 to a dark red calico C square along one side edge as shown. Open seams and press.
4. Stitch another Unit 1 to the opposite side of the dark red calico square to make Row 2 of Block A.
5. With Unit 1 in the reverse position as shown in Figure 3, repeat Steps 1 and 2 to make Row 3 of Block A.

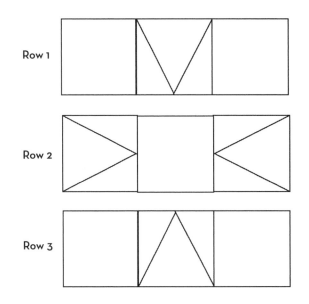

Figure 3. Make rows for Block A.

TO JOIN ROWS FOR BLOCK A

1. Refer to Figure 4. With right sides facing and raw edges aligned, stitch Row 1 and Row 2 together along the bottom edge of Row 1. Open seams and press.
2. With right sides facing and raw edges aligned, stitch Row 2 to Row 3 in the same way.
3. Make 6 of Block A in this way.

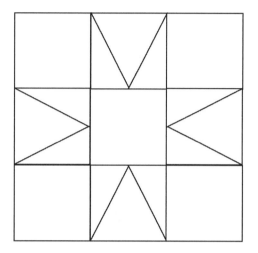

Figure 4. Join rows for Block A.

BLOCK B

This block is made as you made Block A, with different colors. Use the green calico B triangles in place of the black calico B triangles in Unit 1 and black calico C squares in place of green calico C squares.

TO MAKE ROWS OF ALTERNATING A AND B BLOCKS

1. Refer to Figure 5, Row 1. With right sides facing and raw edges aligned, stitch Block A to Block B along the right side edge. Open seams and press.
2. Join another Block A to Block B in the same way to make a row of 3 blocks.
3. Row 2: With right sides facing and raw edges aligned, stitch Block B to Block A. Open seams and press.
4. Next, join another block A to Block B in the same way.
5. Row 3: Repeat Steps 1 and 2.
6. Row 4: Repeat Steps 3 and 4.

Block A   Block B   Block A

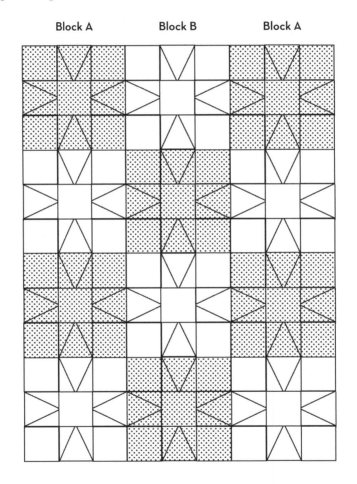

Figure 5. Join rows.

TO JOIN ROWS

1. Refer again to Figure 5. With right sides facing and raw edges aligned, stitch Row 1 to Row 2 along the bottom edge. Open seams and press.
2. Continue to join all 4 rows in this way.

Finished Holiday Quilt.

Figure 6. Add borders.

TO ADD BORDERS

1. Refer to Figure 6. With right sides facing and raw edges aligned, join one bright red calico 2½ × 36½-inch strip to the top edge of the quilt. Open seams and press.
2. Repeat on the bottom edge.
3. With right sides facing and raw edges aligned, join the red calico side border strips in the same way.
4. With right sides facing and raw edges aligned, stitch a green calico 4½ × 40½-inch strip to the top edge of the quilt. Open seams and press.
5. Repeat on the bottom edge.
6. Next, stitch the remaining green calico strips to the sides of the quilt top in the same way. Open seams and press.

TO QUILT

1. With right sides facing and raw edges aligned, stitch the 2 backing pieces together to make a piece 49 × 62 inches.
2. Center the quilt top on the batting and then the backing and pin all 3 layers of fabric together. You will have extra backing fabric all around.
3. Beginning at the center of the quilt top, take long, loose basting stitches in a starburst pattern so there are approximately 6 inches between the lines.
4. To hand-quilt: Take small running stitches along ¼ inch on each side of all seam lines. Do not stitch into the seam allowance all around.
5. To machine-quilt: Set the stitches to approximately 8 stitches per inch. Beginning at the center of the quilt top and working outward, stitch along the seam lines of the patchwork, through all 3 layers of fabric. Do not stitch into the seam allowance all around.
6. Remove pins and basting stitches.

TO FINISH

1. Trim the batting ½ inch smaller than the quilt top all around.
2. Trim the backing to the same size as the quilt top all around.
3. Turn the raw edges of the quilt top ¼ inch to the inside and press. Pin together all around.
4. Machine- or slip-stitch opening closed all around the outside edge of the quilt.

25: HOLIDAY PILLOW

The finished size of this pillow is 18 × 18 inches square. The sizes of the patchwork pieces are the same as the quilt, and all measurements include a ¼-inch seam allowance.

   If you think the Holiday Quilt looks too difficult, begin with the pillow that is made from one block. You will get a feel for how long it takes and whether or not your colors work well with the design.

> **Quilting Club Tip:**
>
> Holiday pillows are great projects for a quilting club. Everyone makes her own project, perhaps using different fabrics, and it's fun to see how each combination of fabrics can look completely different in the same pattern.

MATERIALS

small piece of dark red calico
small piece of dark green calico
¼ yard black or navy calico
¾ yard bright red calico
2 yards red piping
thin quilt batting 19 × 19 inches
18-inch pillow form
16-inch zipper (optional)
tracing paper
cardboard or acetate

DIRECTIONS

1. Trace Patterns A–C (Figure 1, pages 171–72), and transfer to cardboard to make templates. Seam allowance is included.
2. Cut the following:

   From dark red calico:
       1 square using Pattern C

   From dark green calico:
       4 squares using Pattern C

   From black or navy calico:
       Borders:
           2 strips, each 2½ × 14½ inches (top and bottom)
           2 strips, each 2½ × 18½ inches (sides)
       4 triangles using Pattern B

   From bright red calico:
       Borders:
           2 strips, each 1½ × 12½ inches (top and bottom)
           2 strips, each 1½ × 14½ inches (sides)
       1 square, 18½ × 18½ inches for backing
       8 triangles using Pattern A

TO MAKE A SQUARE

1. Refer to Figure 1. With right sides facing and raw edges aligned, stitch a bright red calico A triangle to each diagonal side of a black calico B triangle.
2. Open seams and press. Make 4 pieces squares in this way.

TO MAKE A ROW

1. Refer to Figure 2. With right sides facing and raw edges aligned, stitch a dark green calico C square to the left side edge of a pieced square as shown. Open seams and press.

2. Stitch a dark green calico C square to the right side edge of the pieced square to complete Row 1 of the pillow top. Open seams and press.

3. Row 2: With right sides facing and raw edges aligned, stitch a pieced square to the left side edge of the dark red calico C square as shown. Open seams and press.

4. Complete Row 2 by joining a pieced square to the right side edge of the center square as shown. Open seams and press.

5. Repeat Steps 1 and 2 for Row 3.

TO JOIN ROWS

1. Refer to Figure 3. With right sides facing and raw edges aligned, stitch Row 1 and Row 2 together along the bottom edge. Open seams and press.

2. Join Row 2 and Row 3 in the same way to complete the pillow top as shown.

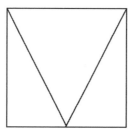

Figure 1. Make a square.

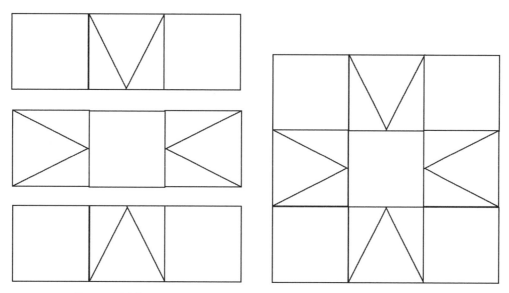

Figure 2. Make rows.

Figure 3. Join rows.

Figures 1 to 3. Make the block.

Holiday Pillow

TO ADD BORDERS

1. Refer to Figure 4. With right sides facing and raw edges aligned, stitch a red 1½ × 12½-inch strip to the top edge of the pillow top. Open seams and press.
2. Repeat on the bottom edge.
3. With right sides facing and raw edges aligned, stitch a bright red 1½ × 14½-inch strip to one side edge of the pillow top. Open seams and press.
4. Repeat with the remaining bright red side strip.
5. With right sides facing and raw edges aligned, stitch a black or navy calico 2½ × 14½-inch strip to the top edge of the pillow top. Open seams and press.
6. Repeat on the bottom edge.
7. With right sides facing and raw edges aligned, stitch a black or navy calico 2½ × 18½-inch strip to one side edge. Open seams and press.
8. Repeat with remaining side strip to complete the patchwork pillow top.

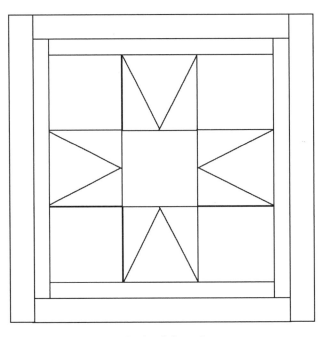

Finished Holiday Pillow.

Figure 4. Add borders.

TO QUILT

1. Center the pillow top over the quilt batting square so there is an equal amount of extra batting all around and pin together.
2. Starting at the center and working outward in a sunburst pattern, baste the fabric together in long loose stitches.
3. To hand-quilt: Using red, black, or green thread, take small running stitches ¼ inch on each side of all seam lines. Do not stitch into the seam allowance all around.
4. To machine-quilt: With a stitch setting at approximately 8 stitches to the inch, stitch along all seam lines. Do not stitch into the seam allowance.
5. When all quilting is complete, remove basting stitches.
6. Trim batting to same size as quilted top.

TO FINISH

1. With raw edges aligned, pin the piping all around the front of the pillow top. Clip into seam allowance of the piping at each corner in order to turn easily.
2. Using a zipper foot on your machine, stitch around as close to the piping as possible.
3. With right sides facing and raw edges aligned, pin the backing to the top of the pillow with the piping between. Using the piping stitches as a guide, stitch around 3 sides and 4 corners, leaving an opening for turning.
4. Trim seam allowance and clip corners. Turn right side out and press.
5. Turn open edges to inside ¼ inch and press. If desired, stitch zipper in place according to package directions.
6. Insert pillow form. If no zipper has been added, slip-stitch opening closed.

Holiday Pillow